WORLD MIGRATION REPORT 2013

D0870773

MIGRANT WELL-BEING AND DEVELOPMENT

International Organization for Migration (IOM)

Contents

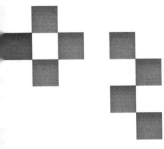

Chapter 3 Review of studies on migration, happiness and well-being

Editorial Team

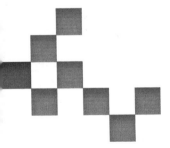

Editors-in-Chief
Frank Laczko
and Gervais Appave

Managing Editors
Shahidul Haque
and Jill Helke

Content Editor
Asmita Naik

Copy Editor
Olga Sheean

Writing Team
Chapter 1: Frank Laczko and Rudolf Anich
Chapter 2: Rudolf Anich, Tara Brian and Frank Laczko
Chapter 3: David Bartram with IOM (Frank Laczko,
        Rudolf Anich and Christine Aghazarm)
Chapter 4: Gallup (Neli Esipova, Anita Pugliese,
        Julie Ray and Kirti Kanitkar)
Chapter 5: Frank Laczko and Gervais Appave

Advisory Support and Editorial Assistance
Christine Aghazarm, David Bartram, Philip Martin,
Susanne Melde and Federico Soda

Publication
Valerie Hagger

Layout
Harvy Gadia

Translators
Carmen Andreu, Fabienne Witt and the TRS team

Executive Assistance
Frances Solinap, Antoinette Wills, Rudolf Anich,
Tara Brian and Christine Aghazarm

Cartography
Tara Brian and Rudolf Anich

Acknowledgements

The Editorial Team wishes to thank all contributing authors and is especially grateful to Mr William Lacy Swing, IOM Director General, for his vision and encouragement in producing this publication.

The Editorial Team is grateful to IOM field offices for their assistance in conducting interviews with migrants for inclusion in the report and to those migrants who agreed to participate. The Team also thanks the authors of the working papers on migrant well-being.

Thanks are also due to David Bartram (University of Leicester), Romina Boarini (OECD) and Philip Martin (UC Davis) for their presentations within the framework of the WMR Seminar Series.

The Editorial Team is particularly grateful to the Governments of Australia, Switzerland and Hungary for their generous financial support towards the development and publication of the *World Migration Report 2013*.

WMR 2013 seminars and working papers

SEMINARS

More than money: Does economic migration bring happiness?
David Bartram,
Senior Lecturer in Sociology at the University of Leicester,
5 September 2012, Geneva, Switzerland.

Measuring progress and well-being: The OECD better life initiative.
Romina Boarini,
Head of the Monitoring Well-Being and Progress Section at the
OECD Statistics Directorate,
1 October 2012, Geneva, Switzerland.

Labour migration and development indicators in the post-2015 global development framework.
Philip Martin,
Professor at the University of California, Davis,
Chair of the UC Comparative Immigration and Integration Program,
10 December 2012, Geneva, Switzerland.

WORKING PAPERS

Migration health, well-being and development: An overview,
by Poonam Dhavan

Migrant well-being in the Middle East and North Africa: A focus on gender in Cairo,
by Harry Cook and Jane Sail

Migrant well-being and development: South America,
by Ezequiel Texidó and Elizabeth Warn

Migrant well-being in South-Eastern Europe, Eastern Europe and Central Asia,
by Marina Manke, Tatjana Dedovic, Katarina Lughofer and Alina Narusova

Migrant well-being: European economic area and Switzerland,
by Anna Platonova

The well-being of economic migrants in South Africa: Health,
gender and development,
by Celine Mazars with Reiko Matsuyama, Jo Rispoli and Jo Vearey

Migrant well-being: Central America, North America and the Caribbean,
by Ricardo Cordero, Salvador Gutierrez and Joan Andreu Serralta

Le bien être des migrants en Afrique de l'ouest [Well-being of migrants in West Africa],
by Geertrui Lanneau and Alexia Scarlett

Boxes, figures, tables and maps

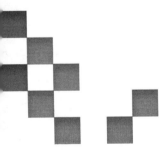

BOXES

MIGRANT VOICES

FIGURES

TABLES

Acronyms

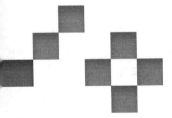

BRICS	Brazil, Russia, India, China, South Africa
DIOC-E	Database on Immigrants in OECD and non-OECD Countries
ESRC	Economic and Social Research Council
ESS	European Social Survey
EU	European Union
Eurostat	Statistical Office of the European Communities
GCC	Gulf Cooperation Council
GDP	Gross domestic product
GFMD	Global Forum on Migration and Development
GMG	Global Migration Group
GNI	Gross national income
GNP	Gross national product
HDI	Human Development Index
HLD	High-level Dialogue on International Migration and Development (United Nations General Assembly)
IBGE	Instituto Brasileiro de Geografia e Estatística [Brazilian Institute for Geography and Statistics]
IDPs	Internally displaced persons
IHDI	Inequality-adjusted Human Development Index
IMF	International Monetary Fund
INE	Instituto Nacional de Estadística [National Statistics Institute] (Spain)
IOM	International Organization for Migration
IPPR	Institute for Public Policy Research
LAC	Latin America and the Caribbean
LDCs	Least developed countries
MDGs	Millennium Development Goals
MNW	Measuring National Well-being programme (UK)
MPI	Migration Policy Institute (USA)
MPI	Multidimensional Poverty Index
MTE	Ministério do Trabalho e Emprego [Ministry of Labour and Employment] (Brazil)
OECD	Organisation for Economic Co-operation and Development
OPHI	Oxford Poverty and Human Development Initiative
SADC	Southern African Development Community
UAE	United Arab Emirates
UIS	UNESCO Institute for Statistics
UNCTAD	United Nations Conference on Trade and Development
UN DESA	United Nations Department of Economic and Social Affairs
UNDP	United Nations Development Programme
UNESCO	United Nations Educational, Scientific and Cultural Organization
UNGA	United Nations General Assembly
UNHCR	United Nations High Commissioner for Refugees
UNODC	United Nations Office on Drugs and Crime
UNRWA	United Nations Relief and Works Agency for Palestine Refugees in the Near East
UNSD	United Nations Statistics Division
WB	World Bank
WMR	*World Migration Report*

Foreword

The *World Migration Report 2013: Migrant Well-being and Development* – the seventh report in IOM's World Migration Report series – focuses on the migrant, and on how migration affects a person's well-being.

While most reports on migration and development look at the impact of remittances sent back home by migrants, this report takes a different approach, exploring how migration affects a person's quality of life and his or her human development across a broad range of dimensions.

The report presents findings from a unique source of data – the Gallup World Poll surveys, conducted in more than 150 countries – allowing for the first-ever assessment of well-being among migrants worldwide. These findings shed new light on how migrants rate their lives, and on how they feel with regard to income, employment, health, security and other dimensions relevant to their well-being.

Furthermore, the *World Migration Report 2013* moves beyond the traditional focus on migrants moving from lower-income countries to more affluent ones, and presents findings for four key migration pathways (from the South to the North, from the North to the South, between countries of the South, and between countries of the North), as well as their implications for development.

The report concludes with a set of recommendations for future initiatives to monitor migrant well-being and the impact of migration on development, with reference to the inclusion of migration in the post-2015 global development framework.

As with previous editions, the *World Migration Report 2013* has benefited from the expertise and experience of IOM colleagues and external scholars. We are particularly grateful for the contribution of the Gallup World Poll team, and also wish to warmly thank the Governments of Australia, Switzerland and Hungary for their generous financial support.

We hope that this report will contribute to the forthcoming discussions at the second United Nations High-level Dialogue (HLD) on International Migration and Development in 2013 and the ongoing debate on the post-2015 global development agenda.

William Lacy Swing
Director General

Overview

Since the first-ever United Nations General Assembly High-level Dialogue (HLD) on International Migration and Development in 2006, there has been increasing international debate about how best to harness the benefits of migration for development. Yet migration remains inadequately integrated into development frameworks at national and local levels, and there is limited public understanding and appreciation of the contribution that migrants make to the development of their countries of origin and destination.

In 2013, a second High-level Dialogue on International Migration and Development will be held, presenting the international community with another opportunity to focus its attention on making migration a positive factor in sustainable development and poverty reduction. The HLD comes at an important time, as the international community moves beyond the Millennium Development Goals and towards the formulation of a post-2015 development agenda.

WMR 2013 draws upon the findings of the Gallup World Poll, using data collected in 2009–2011 from 25,000 first-generation migrants and over 440,000 native-born individuals in over 150 countries, to assess, for the first time, the well-being of migrants worldwide. Most studies on migration tend to focus on the situation of migrants in the North. Gallup's data yield unprecedented global insights into the experience of migrants, providing new evidence of the often understudied situation of migrants in the South.

The key features and messages of *WMR 2013* are presented as a contribution to this ongoing global debate on migration and development, and can be summarized by five key headings:

1. PLACING MIGRANTS AT THE CENTRE OF THE DEBATE

Throughout the history of mankind, human beings have migrated in search of greater opportunities and a better life. While migration is driven by many complex factors, most migrants want to earn a better living, to live in a more agreeable environment or to join family or friends abroad. Many, however, do not move of their own free will but are forced to do so – refugees escaping persecution, for instance; people devastated by conflict or natural disasters; or victims of trafficking. But those who willingly choose to migrate are largely driven by the desire for greater happiness, prosperity and well-being.

Not surprisingly, much research and policy debate has focused on migration as a process and on its socioeconomic impacts in aggregate terms. Many reports on migration and development focus on the broad socioeconomic consequences of migratory processes – studying the impact of, for example, remittances, migrant knowledge networks or diaspora resources. Consequently, the impact of migration on the lives of individual migrants can easily be overlooked. This *World Migration Report 2013* focuses instead on outcome for migrants themselves and on how their lives have been affected in positive or negative ways, as a result of migrating. This approach is consistent with one of the major recommendations of the *WMR 2013* – namely that, instead of being the passive subjects of enquiry, migrants should be given the opportunity to tell their stories. It is hoped that this emphasis on the experiential dimension, as opposed to the usual focus on disembodied socioeconomic dynamics, will open the door to policymaking that is more attuned to human needs.

2. DEVELOPMENT IS ABOUT HUMAN WELL-BEING

The 1986 Declaration on the Right to Development defines development as a "constant improvement of the well-being of the entire population and of all individuals".[1] Similarly, the United Nations Millennium Declaration focuses on the well-being of the individual as the key purpose of development. More recently, the United Nations argued that the notion of well-being and sustainability should be at the core of the global development framework beyond 2015 (UN DESA, 2012a). In this vein, the *WMR 2013* has uniquely framed its approach to assessing development-related outcomes of migration in terms of human well-being. This approach is consistent with recent new orientations in thinking about development that are not limited to economically based notions such as productivity, wealth or income.

Despite the research community's growing interest in developing and testing instruments to measure societal progress from the perspective of human well-being, it is clear that few studies have focused on the well-being of migrants. Those that exist have focused on only one dimension – measures of happiness – and in just a handful of developed countries.

The Gallup World Poll assesses the overall well-being of migrants by asking them questions about objective elements in their lives, such as income level, housing and working conditions, as well as subjective perceptions, feelings and impressions of satisfaction with their lives.

1   www.un.org/documents/ga/res/41/a41r128.htm

3. MIGRATION IS NOT JUST A SOUTH–NORTH PHENOMENON

Traditionally, migration reports and policy discussions about the contribution of migration to development focus on movements from low-/middle-income countries to more affluent ones (such as from the Philippines to the United States). Taking a more inclusive approach, this report sets out to explore whether variations in the origin and destination of migrants can produce different outcomes for those concerned. In addition to South–North migration, therefore, the report covers three other migration pathways: from one high-income country to another (such as from the United Kingdom to Canada: North–North); from a high-income to a low-/middle-income country (such as from Portugal to Brazil: North–South); and from one low-/middle-income country to another (such as from Indonesia to Malaysia: South–South). Based on the research findings, it argues that each of the four migration pathways has specific human development outcomes that have not yet been fully understood or taken into account.

It is clear from the data that a more inclusive approach to migration and development is needed. According to Gallup sources, only 40 per cent of migrants move from South to North. At least one third of migrants move from South to South (although the figure could be higher if more accurate data were available), and just over a fifth of migrants (22%) migrate from North to North. A small but growing percentage of migrants (5%) migrate from North to South. These figures can vary somewhat, depending on which definition of 'North' and 'South' is used.

4. MIGRATION IMPROVES HUMAN DEVELOPMENT, BUT MANY MIGRANTS STILL STRUGGLE TO ACHIEVE SATISFACTORY LEVELS OF WELL-BEING

Comparing the well-being of migrants with that of similar people in the country of origin

This report provides a unique picture of the gains and losses associated with migration. Drawing on the findings of the Gallup World Poll, it examines what migrants have gained and lost through migration, comparing the well-being of migrants who have lived in a destination country for at least five years with estimates of what their lives might have been like had they stayed at home.

The greatest gains are associated with migration to the North, be it North–North or South–North. Migrants in the North generally rate their lives better than do their counterparts in the countries of origin. Long-timer South–North migrants (persons living in a country for five years or more), for example, consider themselves to be better off than they would be back home.

By contrast, migrants in the South tend to rate their lives as similar to, or worse than, those of 'matched stayers' in the home country (persons of a similar profile who did not migrate). Consequently, South–South long-timers consider themselves to be worse off than if they stayed in their home country – reporting, for example, difficulties in obtaining adequate housing, with 27 per cent of them having struggled to afford shelter in the previous year, compared to 19 per cent of their counterparts back home. Migrants from the South generally report that they have more difficulty in achieving a satisfactory standard of living and do not consider themselves to be better off than if they had stayed at home.

It is important to bear in mind that certain vulnerable groups of migrants, such as victims of trafficking, stranded migrants and undocumented migrants, are not identified in the Gallup World Poll.

Comparing the well-being of migrants with that of the native-born

This report also compares the well-being of migrants with that of the native-born in the destination country, highlighting some key differences between the experiences of migrants in the North and South. For example, migrants in the South are less likely than the native-born to report that they are satisfied with their lives. South–South migrants also report that they are less well off, financially, than the native-born. Migrants in the North also face many challenges, but North–North migrants are much less likely than South–North migrants to be struggling to meet their basic needs. Overall, migrants who have moved from one country in the North to another consider themselves to be better off, financially, compared to natives, than do migrants who have moved from South to North. The financial situation of migrants in the North is generally not as good as that of the native-born (although it improves with time) – with 12 per cent of South–North migrants, for instance, finding it very difficult to get by on their incomes, compared to only 6 per cent of the native-born.

The financial challenges faced by migrants are likely due to the difficulties in obtaining work or, if employed, obtaining a full-time job. Migrants in the North are more likely to be unemployed or underemployed: 26 per cent were found to be underemployed and 13 per cent unemployed (compared with 18% and 8%, respectively, of the native-born). In the South, migrants are less likely than the native-born to be part of the official workforce, and just as likely as the native-born to be underemployed or unemployed.

Migrants in the South are less likely than the native-born to feel safe where they live (whereas migrants in the North generally feel as safe as native-born residents). For a minority of migrants in the South, fear and high crime rates prevent them from fully participating socially and economically. However, the situation does seem to improve the longer migrants stay in their new country.

Migrants who have moved to or between countries in the South are less satisfied than the native-born with their personal health and are more likely to have health problems that prevent them from taking part in activities that people their age would normally engage in.

Overall, migrants moving between two high-income countries – or North to North – report the most satisfactory experiences. They have the most positive outcomes in multiple dimensions of well-being, such as life satisfaction, emotional positivity, financial gain, personal safety, community attachment and health. Those migrating between the North and the South, in either direction, have mixed experiences. Generally, economic factors play a key role, with North–South migrants enjoying greater economic prowess and the ability to make their money go further in a relatively cheaper environment. These migrants tend to have fewer social contacts, however, and are less likely to have someone they can count on for help. Conversely, those moving from the South to the North suffer from this economic differential, struggling to make the transition, but they are nevertheless better off for having migrated than those who stayed at home. South/South migrants report relatively little improvement – if any – to their levels of well-being as a result of their having moved. They find it difficult to achieve a satisfactory standard of life, and their outlook for the future is tinged with pessimism. Whereas the migration and policy debate tends to be overwhelmingly focused on the situation of migrants in the North, it is migrants in the South who would appear to be most vulnerable and in need of particular attention.

5. WAY FORWARD AND POST-2015: DEVELOPING A GLOBAL BAROMETER OF MIGRANT WELL-BEING

The shape of the global development agenda beyond 2015 is unknown, but there is growing debate about whether and how migration should be factored into a new global framework. How migration is integrated into the development agenda will depend partly on whether the focus remains on poverty eradication in the poorest countries of the world, rather than on a broader vision of inclusive and sustainable development for all countries.

Whatever approach is taken, there is clearly a need for a much stronger evidence base to understand better on the linkages between migration and development. Additional research and better indicators of migrant well-being are also needed to generate a clearer understanding of the implications of migration for human development in the future.

The poll findings presented in the *WMR 2013* are only a sample of what can be gathered through the Gallup World Poll. By adding new questions to the existing survey, or by increasing migrant sample sizes in certain countries, much more could be learned about the well-being of migrants worldwide. In addition, an ongoing 'Global Migration Barometer' survey could be developed to regularly monitor the well-being of migrants across the globe.

Saving for the future: Peruvian doctor lives and works in Luanda, Angola (South–South)

The street is still muddy from yesterday's rain. In front of the district police headquarters in Bairro Vila Alice in Luanda sits the small clinic where Carlos works as a general physician. Carlos, 32 years old, was born in the city of Trujillo, Peru and migrated two-and-a-half years ago to Angola. After completing medical school in Peru, Carlos worked there for two years as a physician. Through relatives and by chance, he met a Peruvian doctor who had been living in Angola for more than 20 years and was looking to expand his private practice. Although Carlos had never thought about working abroad, he welcomed the opportunity and accepted the assignment.

When Carlos first arrived on the African continent, his assignment was only for one year. However, he chose to extend his contract twice and will soon complete his third year in Angola. "It's a good way to advance my career," he says, "and, with the money saved, we can also make plans for the future – maybe something greater." Carlos notes that living in Angola can be challenging, at times: "Of course, there are the first moments, when you arrive, because of the language barrier, for instance; but then the pollution, the hard task of finding an affordable apartment, and the congestion and transportation problems of Luanda are all little annoyances in the everyday routine." Carlos lives in a good and safe neighbourhood, and says that, in Angola, Peruvian doctors are respected, which has facilitated his integration. Over time, he has managed to make a wide range of friends and contacts, including many Angolans. However, security concerns make it hard to be spontaneous and, as Carlos puts it, "[one's] social life needs to be well organized and all prepared in advance."

Carlos is mainly motivated to remain in Luanda because he enjoys a wide range of responsibilities and a much higher salary than what he would earn in Peru for the same work. This allows him to live comfortably and regularly send money to his family. Carlos is married and the father of a 4-year-old boy. "He was too young for me to bring here. For an adult, it's okay here but, for children, it's more difficult because the sanitary environment and the education are not adequate," says Carlos, confessing that living away from his family is the main difficulty he faces. While the remittances sent home help pay for his family's daily life in Peru, Carlos made the decision to migrate primarily to save for the future and to be able to offer greater opportunities to his son and wife. In Carlos's own words: "We have a child and we must think about his future. By being here, I have achieved some very good objectives, in terms of money and savings."

Technology makes life a bit easier, enabling Carlos to talk to his wife and son every day through a video call. They have only seen each other three times since he moved to Angola. When asked where he would like to be in a few years' time, Carlos's eyes roam around his small desk and land on a picture of his son: "This is a big decision about family reunion. I could go back to Peru for a specialization, I could move to a different country, or I could stay in Angola, but I want to be with my family." Carlos concludes that, while he had never imagined living outside of his country and it has not been easy living away from his loved ones, he doesn't regret his decision to migrate.

Chapter 1

Introduction

Frank Laczko and Rudolf Anich

HIGHLIGHTS

For thousands of years, human beings have migrated in search of a better life. Migration is the result of numerous factors; many migrate in search of greater opportunities – to earn a better living, to live in a more agreeable environment or to join family or friends abroad. Of course, a considerable portion of migrants do not choose to move but are forced to flee their homes against their will – refugees escaping persecution, people devastated by conflict or natural disaster, or victims of trafficking. But for those who do choose to migrate, the most fundamental issues are whether they will be happier if they migrate and whether life will be better than it was before. This report, based on the first global study of its kind, seeks to answer these universal questions, in the context of migration as a means of achieving individual betterment and growth.

Migration is not purely a personal matter, however, as it can also affect economic development. Policymakers are increasingly aware that the migration of individuals has a cumulative effect, nationally, and that it can have an impact on the economic health of both the country of origin and the country of destination. Migration can result in a chain of development – from individuals, through to households, communities and, ultimately, countries. Globalization has led to a significant increase in human mobility, with social, economic and environmental implications for all concerned.

Traditionally, policy discussions about how migration can contribute to development have focused on movements from low-/middle-income countries to high-income ones – for example, from the Philippines to the United States of America. (This type of migration will hereinafter be referred to as 'South–North'.) This report takes a broader approach, focusing on movements of people in all directions: migration between high-income countries – for example, from the United Kingdom to Canada (hereinafter referred to as 'North–North'); movements from high- to low-/middle-income countries – for example, from Portugal to Brazil (hereinafter referred to as 'North–South'); and migration from one low-/middle-income country to another – for example, from Indonesia to Malaysia (hereinafter referred to as 'South–South'). It argues that all four migration pathways have consequences for development, which need to be taken into account. The report adopts the terminology used in development discourse to categorize countries according to their economic status, whereby 'North' refers to high-income countries and 'South' to low- and middle-income countries.

Governments are increasingly paying attention to the well-being of populations. The global economic crisis highlighted the need for more sustainable ways of living, while prompting the realization that economic growth alone is not a sufficient barometer for measuring societal progress. This report presents original research on migrant well-being worldwide, clearly demonstrating, for the first time, the importance of such well-being to the long-term sustainability of both economic development and migration itself.

This chapter looks at the linkages between migration and development and how this issue has, in recent years, increasingly been brought to the international policy agenda. It identifies the specific contribution of this report to the prevailing thinking on migration and development. The chapter concludes with a guide to the report, describing the research methodology used, explaining classification and terminology, and setting out some caveats to bear in mind when reading this report. It also outlines the report structure.

MIGRATION AND THE DEVELOPMENT AGENDA

While migration clearly has consequences for migrants and their families, migration can also affect the development of economies. Policymakers are increasingly aware that the migration of individuals has a cumulative effect, nationally, and that it can have an impact on economic growth. Migration can result in a chain of development – from individuals, through to households, communities and, ultimately, countries. Although migrants 'give back' to their home countries, it is usually in the form of private remittances to individuals and households. Yet such activities have wider implications: for example, money sent back to family members may enable them to invest in a new home, thereby boosting employment in the construction sector in that locality; or a person returning to their country of origin after studying abroad may bring back skills that benefit society in general.

Not all migration effects are positive, however. Migration may, for instance, drive inflation if remittances boost spending power without increasing productivity, or it could harm important economic sectors such as education and health care through 'brain drain'. Whether migration leads to positive developmental effects depends on a complex interplay of factors, such as: the circumstances in the countries of origin and destination; the reason for leaving and, critically, whether the move was voluntary; and the pattern of migration (Global Migration Group, 2010). There may be negative effects at the household level, too – for example, through the separation and dislocation of families.

An individual's decision to migrate may be motivated by a range of factors:

- **Economic factors**: The growing gap in living standards and wages between countries acts as a magnet (referred to as a 'pull factor'), drawing migrants towards countries with higher standards of living or with greater economic growth and employment opportunities.

- **Governance and public services**: Poor governance, corruption and a lack of good-quality education and health services are 'push factors', prompting international migration.

- **Demographic imbalances**: These can take various forms – for instance, decreasing fertility rates and increasing life expectancy in many high-income countries, which contribute to an imbalance in supply and demand for labour between developed and developing regions. Labour surpluses in lower- and middle-income countries can create underemployment, which can create incentives to migrate. On the other hand, the aging population in most high-income industrialized countries considerably increases the demand for foreign workers.

- **Conflict**: The number of refugees under the mandate of the United Nations High Commissioner for Refugees (UNHCR) was over 10 million in 2012, and numbers of internally displaced persons (IDPs) reached 28.8 million (UNHCR, 2013). Conflicts can be ethnic and/or religious in nature, but they may also be the result of economic inequality or competition for natural resources. Linked to this, the absence of personal freedom (be it in thought, religion or other) can be a motivator, as can discrimination, based on race, ethnicity, gender, religion or other grounds.[2]

2 Numbers of refugees and internally displaced people (IDPs) also include those who migrate because of natural disasters or other events that do not involve conflict.

- **Environmental factors**: The numbers of people moving as a result of environmental factors such as earthquakes, industrial accidents, floods, soil/coastal erosion and droughts, some of which may be related to climate change, are on the rise. Population movements induced by environmental factors tend to be predominantly internal.

- **Transnational networks**: The emergence of organized migrant communities in destination countries constitutes a social and cultural 'pull factor'. A network of family members abroad can further promote migration as it facilitates the migration process for others, and such movements account for the bulk of the legal migration flows in many industrialized countries.

In addition, the patterns of movement also ultimately influence whether migration has positive development effects, and would include:

- **Types of movements** – permanent or temporary;

- **Status of the migrants** – regular or irregular;

- **Protection of rights** – the extent to which migrants' rights are protected;

- **Planning** – planned or unplanned nature of the flows;

- **Scale** – a small percentage of a population moving over a lengthy period of time, or a mass movement of people over a short period of time;

- **Socioeconomic background** – gender, age and marital status. The demographic and socioeconomic profiles of migrants have important implications for development in countries of origin and destination. They affect the labour market (in terms of the availability of skilled versus unskilled workers); the population structure (for example, in terms of the proportion of young versus old people, married versus single migrants); and the need for, and provision of, services (given that migrant flows may include children who require education, or workers who supply health-care services). Whether migrants move with their families or alone, and the circumstances of household members left behind (who, for example, may need to make arrangements for the care of children), also make a difference.

Since IOM published its first *World Migration Report* in the year 2000, the topic of migration and development has come to the fore, resulting in a more sophisticated appreciation of the connections between the two. Traditionally, migration has been viewed primarily as a problem arising from a lack of development, or it has been regarded negatively, due to fears about a possible 'brain drain' among skilled workers. Today, there is growing recognition that migration can contribute to development, if properly harnessed and effectively managed by policymakers.

Development can be defined as "a process of improving the overall quality of life of a group of people and, in particular, expanding the range of opportunities open to them", according to *Mainstreaming Migration into Development Planning: A Handbook for policy-makers and practitioners*, initiated by IOM and published by the Global Migration Group (GMG, 2010). The focus of this definition is on human development, rather than on the traditionally recognized indicators, which relate primarily to economic growth and are measured in gross domestic product (GDP) or gross national income (GNI). Advancing human development means exploring all avenues to improve a person's opportunities and freedoms, whether income-

or non-income-related. This can include, for example, improvements to people's lives such as expanded access to social services, reduced vulnerability to risk, and increased political participation (GMG, 2010:10).

It is important to remember, however, that the concept of human development does not apply solely to the poorest countries of the world, or only to movements of people to more affluent countries. North–North migration (for instance, a German doctor moving to the United States) or North–South migration (for example, a skilled Portuguese worker migrating to Angola) can contribute significantly to development in both the country of origin and the country of destination. Development benefits generated from these types of movements are too often overlooked in the development discourse.

In recent years, migration and its linkages to development have become an increasingly important policy issue. The first United Nations High-level Dialogue (HLD) on International Migration and Development, held in 2006, firmly established migration on the development agenda and led to the creation of the Global Forum on Migration and Development (GFMD) in 2007. The GFMD has served as an important platform for improving dialogue between States on migration and development, and this debate will continue to gain prominence in a number of forthcoming policy forums:

2013 – The second United Nations High-level Dialogue (HLD) on International Migration and Development presents a critical opportunity for the international community to improve the alignment of migration and development policies.

2014 – A United Nations review of the twentieth anniversary of the implementation of the International Conference on Population and Development (ICPD) programme of action will have implications for international and internal migration.

2015 – Post-2015 United Nations Development Agenda discussions will consider the shape of the global development framework beyond 2015 – the deadline for the achievement of the Millennium Development Goals (MDGs), in which migration is a key factor.

CONTRIBUTION OF THE REPORT

The *WMR 2013* is intended to contribute to the global debate on development in three distinct ways:

- **By focusing attention on all pathways of migratory movement**. Traditionally, the focus has been on migration from low-/middle-income countries to more affluent ones, but this report considers three additional migration pathways – migration between low-/middle-income countries or between high-income ones, and migration from the rich, industrialized world to countries that are relatively poorer – as well as their implications for development.

- **Shifting the focus onto the well-being of migrants and their quality of life**, rather than focusing on remittances and the impact of migration on economic life and trade, as has been the case in the past.

- **Contributing to the debate about how to factor migration into the post-2015 framework for development**. Despite the growing interest in migration and development, the issue has not been factored into the MDGs or systematically integrated into national development plans.

Four migration pathways

Over the last decade, numerous reports and studies have been published on the linkages between migration and development. Typically, the migration and development policy discourse and related studies focus on the implications of migration for development when a person moves from South to North. This skews the policy debate and draws attention away from other migration flows that merit equal attention. In fact, less than half of all international migrants move from South to North, and almost as many move between countries of the South (see chapter 2 for details). This report looks at migration and development from a broader perspective, considering the implications for development and well-being when people move in other directions as well.

The report adopts the terminology used in development discourse to categorize countries according to their economic status. As mentioned above, broadly speaking, 'North' refers to high-income countries and 'South' to low- and middle-income countries, as classified by the World Bank. Such labels have their limitations, however, with different definitions of 'North' and 'South' producing varying results regarding the magnitude and characteristics of migration along each of the four pathways. In addition, both 'North' and 'South' encompass a wide range of different migrant situations and categories (as discussed later in chapter 1 and also in chapter 2). Nonetheless, this division is useful for looking at migration and development in a more holistic way. For the time being, the key point to note is that this report looks at all migration pathways, whether they are South–North, South–South, North–South or North–North.

South–South migrants are economically important, due to the magnitude of numbers and the potential scale of remittances, but their life experiences are a largely understudied area. This 'blind spot' for policymakers largely reflects the lack of reliable data on migrants who move from one developing country to another, but also the heavy emphasis on South–North flows in policy debates and research.

Migrant well-being

Many reports on migration and development focus on the impact of remittances on development, or on the wider impact of migration on trade and the economy. This report looks instead at the relationship between the migrant and development, and how migration affects a person's quality of life and their well-being. Many migrants, especially economic migrants, choose to move abroad in search of a better life – effectively, to improve their well-being. But are they better off, as a result? How do their lives compare with those who did not migrate? How does their well-being compare with that of the people in the country they have moved to? These are some of the questions that this report seeks to answer.

Policy interest

This enquiry takes place within the context of a growing interest among policymakers and scholars in measuring the happiness and well-being of populations. This is especially evident in high-income countries, but is also increasingly a concern in low- and middle-income countries – for example, the Fourth OECD World Economic Forum, held in Delhi in October 2012, focused on the theme of 'development and well-being' (see also Gough and McGregor, 2007). Indeed, the Himalayan Kingdom of Bhutan was the first to use measures of 'gross national happiness' as a way of assessing social progress and, in April 2012, Bhutan hosted a high-level meeting at the United Nations in New York, bringing together over 800 participants to discuss the creation of an economic paradigm that serves human happiness and well-being of all life (Royal Government of Bhutan, 2012). The global economic crisis and the challenge of maintaining economic stability has highlighted the need for more sustainable ways of living. In addition, emerging evidence from academia suggests that economic wealth does not necessarily generate well-being among the population, affirming popular notions that 'money does not buy happiness'. In its 2011 report, *How's Life: Measuring well-being*, the Organisation for Economic Co-operation and Development (OECD) referred to the discrepancy between macroeconomic indicators and the real-life experience of ordinary people:

> In recent years, concerns have emerged regarding the fact that macro-economic statistics, such as GDP, did not portray the right image of what ordinary people perceived about the state of their own socioeconomic conditions... Addressing such perceptions of the citizens is of crucial importance for the credibility and accountability of public policies but also for the very functioning of democracy (OECD, 2011).

Interest in the subject of well-being was given a boost by the report of the Commission on the Measurement of Economic Performance and Social Progress, established by the former French President Nicolas Sarkozy. The Commission, which was led by Nobel Prize-winning economists Joseph E. Stiglitz and Amartya Sen, along with French economist Jean-Paul Fitoussi, recognized the limitations of measuring societal progress and development in terms of economic measures such as gross national product (GNP) or GDP, and made the case for the collection of a wider set of well-being indicators to assess whether economies were serving the needs of society (Stiglitz, Sen and Fitoussi, 2009). A similar 'national well-being project' is underway in the United Kingdom, comprised of an extensive survey to measure and analyse a wide range of dimensions and determinants of well-being (Dolan et al., 2011). The OECD, in its aforementioned report, includes a 'Better Life Index' that measures subjective well-being (OECD, 2011).

These examples reflect an increasing recognition of the need to find new ways of measuring social progress, and the fact that GDP, long a key point of reference for economic policy and development, may have severe limitations as an indicator of well-being (see, for example, Boarini et al., 2006), especially insofar as it fails to capture the *subjective* dimensions of well-being – namely, what people actually experience and feel about their lives. The United Nations calls for a more holistic approach to development, arguing that the notion of well-being and sustainability should be at the core of the post-2015 goals and indicators (UN DESA, 2012a), but internationally agreed standards on such non-economic indicators have yet to be developed (Boarini et al., 2006:6).

Well-being defined

There are different definitions of the term well-being. This report uses the definition developed by Gallup, since it is responsible for the original research findings on which this report is based. In *Wellbeing: The Five Essential Elements*, Gallup scientists identify career, social connections, personal economics, health, and community as the main contributors to a person's overall subjective well-being.

Other terms to describe well-being, such as quality of life, living standards, human development and happiness, have been used in various academic studies and, sometimes, interchangeably. In fact, well-being is a broader concept, encompassing a number of different dimensions. It can be measured by asking people how they feel and their perceptions about different aspects of their lives, such as job satisfaction, personal relationships and community attachment. It can also be measured through the collection and verification of objective data such as employment rates, salary levels, life expectancy and housing conditions.

It might be expected that a person with higher scores on objective criteria would be happier – that objective well-being correlates with *subjective* well-being or happiness. This may often be the case since, for example, being ill makes most people unhappy, while having opportunities for education may be seen as deeply satisfying. However, the linkages between objective and subjective well-being are quite complex and convergence is not complete, as suggested by the subtitle of a recent book by the economist Carol Graham (2009): The paradox of happy peasants and unhappy millionaires. There is a need for further enquiry into the factors that contribute to subjective well-being; what types of development are best for a population's well-being; and whether some forms of development make people less happy even if it increases their objective assets.

Future development framework

This report also seeks to make a contribution to the forthcoming debate on the future development agenda after 2015 – the deadline for the achievement of the MDGs. With globalization, human mobility has increased significantly since the MDGs were adopted in the year 2000. Migration has emerged as a significant factor in the achievement of all three pillars of sustainable development – economic, social and environmental development – and an important factor in forthcoming discussions. Specifically, voluntary, safe, legal and orderly migration can generate significant human and societal development gains; equally, migration that is forced, involuntary, massive or unplanned (whether as a result of conflict, natural disaster, environmental degradation, rights violations or severe lack of economic and livelihood opportunities) can have significant negative repercussions for human and societal development. A recent United Nations report, *Realizing the Future We Want for All*, provides a first outline for a system-wide vision and elements of a road map in anticipation of these discussions (UN, 2012). IOM and the United Nations Department of Economic and Social Affairs (UN DESA) contributed a 'think piece' to highlight the importance of keeping migration in the foreground of these development debates (IOM and UN DESA, 2012).

Despite the growing international focus on migration and development, migration as a topic is not factored into the MDGs or systematically integrated into national development plans. One of the reasons for this is the lack of reliable data. There has also been reluctance among those who work in the migration and development arena to focus too much on developing agreed targets and indicators. In the GFMD, for example, there is a concern that investing in this area might undermine the informal and non-binding forms of cooperation that have developed within the GFMD. States do not wish to take formal responsibility for achieving an agreed set of migration and development targets each year. Thus there has been relatively little monitoring of the extent to which existing migration and development goals are being achieved.

The future global development framework will likely need to include better indicators of how migration affects development and, particularly, migrant well-being, if migration is to be factored into the global development agenda in a meaningful way. How this could be done is considered in the concluding chapter of this report. The Gallup World Poll is a unique source of data on the living and working conditions of migrants, providing a means of exploring whether human development indicators for migrants are improving.

GUIDE TO THE REPORT

Sources of information

WMR 2013 draws on a variety of primary and secondary sources of data to determine whether migration leads to improved personal circumstances for migrants. It explores the wider implications of this for the achievement of sustainable development, presenting original findings from the Gallup World Poll on migrant well-being, reviewing relevant literature, providing an analysis of migration trends, and shedding new light on how migrants rate their lives. The results are not presented by country or region but are categorized by the direction of travel, according to the four migration pathways that reflect the movement of people from South to South, from South to North, from North to North, and from North to South.

Gallup World Poll

While the global community has been moving towards a broader perception of 'development' as the organized pursuit of 'well-being', little research has focused on migrants. The well-being of migrants affects not only their ability to fully participate in society but also their ability to send home remittances, and to acquire skills and knowledge that could be useful if they choose to return to their country of origin. Research to date has focused on migrant populations in specific countries or regions only. The findings of the Gallup World Poll present, for the first time, an opportunity to assess the well-being of migrants worldwide.

Using data on well-being from 25,000 first-generation migrants and over 440,000 native-born individuals collected between 2009 and 2011 in over 150 countries, the Gallup World Poll provides unique insights into the living and working conditions and perceptions of migrants in the world today. The poll gathered evidence using indicators such as income, unemployment and underemployment, happiness, satisfaction with health, and feelings of security.

It is important to note, however, that the Gallup World Poll provides an aggregate picture of the well-being of migrants. There are many subgroups of the migrant population – stranded migrants, victims of trafficking, unaccompanied minors, migrants in an irregular situation – who are not identified in the Gallup World Poll. This may be because the group in question represents a small subsample of the migrant population surveyed, or the questions in the survey did not distinguish between, for example, documented and undocumented migrants.

In addition, there are many groups of migrants around the world who face human rights abuses and exploitation, and who live in very vulnerable situations. For more information, see, for example, the *Global Trafficking in Persons Report* (US Department of State, 2012 and box 1 of this report). The well-being of migrants can also be adversely affected when significant numbers of people are displaced due to environmental factors or when a conflict occurs. Such situations are not easily captured by the Gallup World Poll and, hence, are not specifically discussed in this report. Nonetheless, the findings on well-being presented here do not in any way deny or undermine the egregious conditions experienced by many migrant groups.

This report analyses migrant well-being in several ways. Firstly, it compares the self-reported well-being of migrants (those who have recently migrated as well as long-timers – those who have lived in the destination country for more than five years) with the self-reported well-being of the native-born residents. Secondly, it investigates what migrants have gained and lost by migrating abroad, using a statistical model that compares the lives of migrants with those of a matched sample of people of the same age, gender and education profile in the country of origin who have not migrated.

 Box 1

Young woman trafficked from the Russian Federation to the Middle East

Irina was a 16-year-old highschool student living in the Russian Federation when she accepted a family friend's proposal to take a quick trip to the Middle East. The offer of USD 500 for her help in bringing back merchandise to sell back home was appealing and, within days, she was introduced to a broker who gave her a passport, a tourist visa and a plane ticket. The broker then announced that the travel agenda had been "improved": she was now to work as a waitress in a local café for USD 1,000 a month. Irina's mother was suspicious but was quickly assured that her daughter was in good hands. Also, she was told that the travel arrangements had cost the broker a lot of money and that cancellation would mean they owed him USD 1,000. Upon arrival at her destination, Irina found that she was not be a waitress, but was expected to work as a prostitute. Her passport was taken away and she was threatened with violence if she refused to obey or tried to run away.

Irina's life became a series of hotel rooms, boarding houses, 'madams' and clients, until she finally tried to escape. She stole her documents and some cash and ran away. Upon reaching the airport, however, she was stopped by the police. The madam was with them and claimed that Irina had stolen her money. Without asking questions, the police ordered Irina to return with the madam. She was resold to another hotel-owner and saddled with a new debt of USD 10,000 to compensate for her misbehaviour. News from the Russian Federation of the broker's arrest, following a petition by Irina's mother, brought added threats and abuse. But Irina did not give up trying to escape. Six months into her ordeal, she finally managed to contact the Russian Embassy. There, she found out that her name had remained on the Interpol 'missing persons' files for months. She was assisted by the Russian Federation Embassy, IOM and the United Nations Office on Drugs and Crime (UNODC) in returning home and reintegrating back into her community.

Classification and terminology

This section of the report explains in further detail how the terms 'North' and 'South' are used when they refer to the four migration pathways. It reviews the different definitions used by various international agencies, and considers the implications of these different definitions for the understanding of international migration trends.

Conceptualization of 'North' and 'South'

The North–South divide between wealthy developed economies and poorer developing countries has been referred to in public debates since the early 1960s,[3] but the use of the terms 'North' and 'South' became much more prevalent after the fall of the Berlin wall in 1989. Indeed, after the subsequent dissolution of the Soviet Union, the term 'Second World' lost significance and ultimately led to a simplification of the global world order, whereby the First World became the 'North' and the Third World became the 'South' (Thérien, 1999; Reuveny and Thompson, 2007).

To date, there is no agreement on how best to categorize countries in accordance with the North–South dichotomy. In fact, 'North' and 'South' do not exist, as such, but are only artificial constructs intended to reflect the current global situation with regard to a specific dimension of development. Other ways of categorizing and indexing countries have also been developed (see box 2 on page 47). Moreover, the use of 'North' and 'South' in this context has not captured the popular imagination. In many countries, the terms are used to describe internal divides (for example, in the United Kingdom, they are used in the opposite sense, with the South seen as having greater economic prospects than the relatively impoverished North). In addition, the general public tends to see 'North' and 'South' as a spatial and geographic division of the world, not as an economic

---

3   Notably, the terms 'North' and 'South' were used in the Brandt Reports in 1980 and 1983 (reports of the *Independent Commission on International Development Issues*, first chaired by Willy Brandt, former West German Chancellor, in 1980), calling for a transfer of resources from developed to developing economies to end poverty and promote development. Earlier, the *Brandt Line* was a first attempt to divide world economies into 'North' and 'South' – namely, developed and developing countries.

one, which can lead to confusion; for instance, many countries in the 'North' may actually be situated in the geographical south and vice versa (as, for example, Australia).

The purpose of using the North–South classification in this report is to simplify the situation in order to better understand overall global trends. As with all categorizations, classifications and indexes, the greater the number of dimensions that are taken into account when developing a categorization, the more accurate the resulting picture will be. Putting all countries into two categories only – namely, 'North' and 'South' – inevitably means that there will be exceptions.

The North–South dichotomy only works if it is understood that the situation in each group is not homogenous. Indeed, grouping countries into 'North' and 'South' or into four migration pathways, based on the indicators described in this chapter, does not take into account the relevant sociocultural differences among migrants. As highlighted by Bakewell (2009), it is important to keep in mind that, within broad groupings such as 'South' and 'North', there are many divergent groups of migrants with different sociocultural backgrounds and migration experiences. Compare, for example:

- Unemployed Portuguese youth going to Brazil and Europeans investing and working in India (North–South)
- European Union (EU) students studying abroad and Estonians seeking job opportunities in Finland (North–North)
- Guatemalan seasonal workers in Canada and domestic workers from the Philippines moving to Saudi Arabia (South–North)

While the North–South divide might not accurately capture an evolving development reality,[4] it is still a useful means of capturing policymakers' attention, by simplifying the way in which migration trends are presented, and helping to show how migration patterns between developed and developing countries can vary. The use of terms such as 'South–South migration' has helped to change the migration and development debate by encouraging policymakers to acknowledge that much migration occurs between developing countries.

Three main categorizations

This report draws on the three most commonly used categorizations provided by the United Nations Department of Economic and Social Affairs (UN DESA), the World Bank (WB) and the United Nations Development Programme (UNDP). Table 1 provides an overview of all countries defined as part of the 'North' and 'South' in 2010, using the three key classifications (see also map 1, on page 46).

4   As Cox and Sinclair (1996) point out, the North seems to produce its own internal South while, in the South, a selected part of the population is economically integrated with the North.

United Nations Department of Economic and Social Affairs (UN DESA) classification

This classification groups countries into developing and developed regions:[5]

- North includes Northern America,[6] Europe, Japan, Australia and New Zealand (a total of 56 countries).
- South is composed of Africa, the Americas (without the United States and Canada), the Caribbean, Asia (except Japan), and Oceania (except Australia and New Zealand).
- Using this definition, the 'North' does not include the OECD countries Chile, Israel, Mexico, the Republic of Korea, and Turkey, or high-income non-OECD countries such as Bahrain; Hong Kong, China; Puerto Rico; or the United Arab Emirates. Instead, several countries in Eastern Europe (such as Belarus, the Republic of Moldova, the Russian Federation and Ukraine) are considered part of the 'North'.
- The UN DESA classification comes from the United Nations Statistics Division (UNSD) and is based on statistical convenience and has not changed significantly over time.

World Bank classification

This classifies countries every year according to their income level – the GNI per capita.

- Countries are divided into four groups (low-, lower-middle-, upper-middle- and high-income).[7]
- 'North' is composed of countries belonging to the high-income group. Compared to the UN DESA definition, this definition encompasses a greater number of countries (70, in 2010), also including the following: Bahrain; Barbados; China; Hong Kong, China; Israel; Macao, China; Oman; Puerto Rico; Qatar; the Republic of Korea; Saudi Arabia; Singapore; Trinidad and Tobago; and the United Arab Emirates.
- However, as stressed by the World Bank, the term high-income "is not intended to imply that all economies in the group are experiencing similar development or that other economies have reached a preferred or final stage of development. Classification by income does not necessarily reflect development status."[8]

UNDP classification

This classification adopts a broader development approach and uses the Human Development Index (HDI)[9] as the criterion for distinguishing countries based on health (life expectancy at birth), educational aspects (mean and expected years of schooling) and income.

---

5   There is no established convention for the designation of 'developed' or 'developing' countries or areas in the United Nations system. See: http://unstats.un.org/unsd/methods/m49/m49regin.htm.
6   In the UN DESA classification, Northern America includes Bermuda, Canada, Greenland, Saint Pierre and Miquelon, and the United States of America. Countries such as Belize, Costa Rica, El Salvador, Guatemala, Honduras, Mexico, Nicaragua and Panama are part of Central America. See: http://unstats.un.org/unsd/methods/m49/m49.htm.
7   According to the 2010 GNI per capita, the groups are defined as follows: low-income – USD 1,005 or less; lower-middle-income – USD 1,006–3,975; upper-middle-income – USD 3,976–12,275; high-income – USD 12,276 or more. See: http://wdronline.worldbank.org/worldbank/a/incomelevel.
8   See: http://wdronline.worldbank.org/worldbank/a/incomelevel.
9   The UNDP Human Development Index is a way of measuring development by combining indicators of life expectancy, educational attainment and income into a composite single statistic that serves as a frame of reference for both social and economic development. HDI sets a minimum and a maximum for each dimension, called goalposts, and then shows where each country stands in relation to these goalposts, expressed as a value between 0 and 1. See http://hdr.undp.org/en/statistics/hdi/ for more details.

• In 2010, 42 countries reached a very high HDI were thus considered to be developed countries or the 'North'.[10] The categorization resulting from the HDI corresponds more closely to the one used by the World Bank, whereby the 'North' includes most high-income countries in Latin America, the Middle East and Asia (not included in the UN DESA definition). Nonetheless, compared to the World Bank categorization, the total number of countries defined as being part of the 'North' is significantly lower, mainly due to the non-inclusion of small (island) States.

 Table 1   **'North' and 'South' as defined by UN DESA, the World Bank and UNDP, 2010**

UN DESA	World Bank	UNDP
'South' includes five developing regions: Africa; the Americas (excluding Northern America); the Caribbean; Asia (excluding Japan); and Oceania (excluding Australia and New Zealand).	**'South'** includes low- and middle-income countries.	**'South'** includes countries ranking low, medium and high on the HDI.
'North' includes countries/territories in the developed regions: Albania; Andorra; Australia; Austria; Belarus; Belgium; Bermuda; Bosnia and Herzegovina; Bulgaria; Canada; Channel Islands; Croatia; Czech Republic; Denmark; Estonia; Faeroe Islands; Finland; France; Germany; Gibraltar; Greece; Greenland; Holy See; Hungary; Iceland; Ireland; Isle of Man; Italy; Japan; Latvia; Liechtenstein; Lithuania; Luxembourg; Malta; Monaco; Montenegro; Netherlands; New Zealand; Norway; Poland; Portugal; Republic of Moldova; Romania; Russian Federation; Saint Pierre and Miquelon; San Marino; Serbia; Slovakia; Slovenia; Spain; Sweden; Switzerland; The former Yugoslav Republic of Macedonia; Ukraine; United Kingdom of Great Britain and Northern Ireland; and the United States of America.	**'North'** includes high-income countries/territories: Andorra, Aruba; Australia; Austria; Bahamas; Bahrain; Barbados; Belgium; Bermuda; Brunei Darussalam; Canada; Cayman Islands; Channel Islands; Croatia; Curaçao; Cyprus; Czech Republic; Denmark; Equatorial Guinea; Estonia; Faeroe Islands; Finland; France; French Polynesia; Germany; Gibraltar; Greece; Greenland; Guam; Hong Kong, China; Hungary; Iceland; Ireland; Isle of Man; Israel; Italy; Japan; Kuwait; Liechtenstein; Luxembourg; Macao, China; Malta; Mariana Islands; Monaco; Netherlands; New Caledonia; New Zealand; Norway; Oman; Poland; Portugal; Republic of Korea; Puerto Rico; Qatar; Saint Maarten (Dutch part); San Marino; Saudi Arabia; Singapore; Slovakia; Slovenia; Spain; St Martin (French part); Sweden; Switzerland; Trinidad and Tobago; Turks and Caicos Islands; United Arab Emirates; United Kingdom of Great Britain and Northern Ireland; the United States of America; and the Virgin Islands (US).	**'North'** include countries/territories ranking very high on the HDI: Andorra; Australia; Austria; Bahrain; Barbados; Belgium; Brunei Darussalam; Canada; Cyprus; Czech Republic; Denmark; Estonia; Finland; France; Germany; Greece; Hong Kong, China; Hungary; Iceland; Ireland; Israel; Italy; Japan; Liechtenstein; Luxembourg; Malta; Netherlands; New Zealand; Norway; Poland; Portugal; Qatar; Republic of Korea; Singapore; Slovakia; Slovenia; Spain; Sweden; Switzerland; United Arab Emirates; United Kingdom of Great Britain and Northern Ireland; and the United States of America.

Sources: UN DESA: http://unstats.un.org/unsd/methods/m49/m49.htm
World Bank: http://wdronline.worldbank.org/worldbank/a/incomelevel
UNDP: http://hdr.undp.org/en/statistics/hdi/

10 The HDI initially divided countries into three groups (low-, medium- and high-income). The category of a country was determined by absolute cut-off values. Recent improvements introduced the very high HDI category, reduced the amount of variation within each group, and made cut-off values more relative. For more information, please see: http://hdr.undp.org/en/statistics/understanding/issues/.

UN DESA

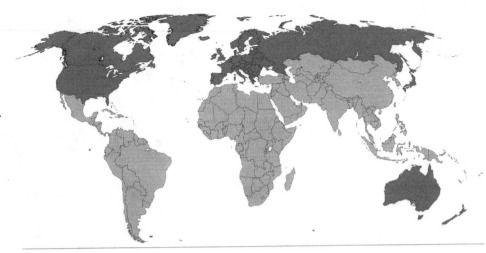

World Bank

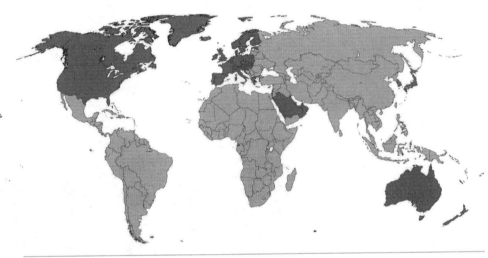

UNDP

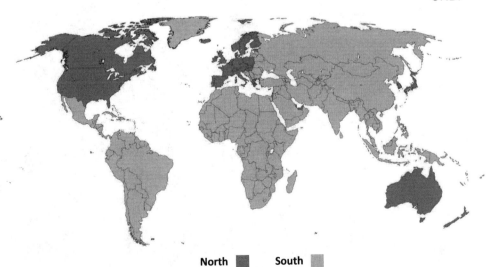

North ▪   **South** ▪

Sources: UN DESA: http://unstats.un.org/unsd/methods/m49/m49.htm
World Bank: http://wdronline.worldbank.org/worldbank/a/incomelevel
UNDP: http://hdr.undp.org/en/statistics/hdi/

Note: The boundaries and names shown and the designations used on these maps do not imply
official endorsement or acceptance by the International Organization for Migration (IOM).
Dotted lines are used to indicate administrative boundaries, undetermined boundaries
and situations where the final boundary has not yet been determined.

Box 2

New ways of classifying countries

Current definitions designate a country as being in the North or the South, based on the average national value for a specific indicator, but other methods are being developed to capture more subtle differences.

1. Measures to show differences within countries.

The North–South classification does not sufficiently capture inequalities within a country, especially one with a large population (for example, Brazil and China, which have emerging economies). The Inequality-adjusted HDI (IHDI) introduced by UNDP in the *Human Development Report 2010* aims to address this aspect by measuring the level of human development of people in a society that accounts for inequality.[11] Likewise, the Multidimensional Poverty Index (MPI),[12] developed by the Oxford Poverty and Human Development Initiative (OPHI) and UNDP, provides a multidimensional picture of people living in poverty.

2. Measures based on detailed economic indicators.

The International Monetary Fund (IMF), in its World Economic Outlook (WEO) database, classifies the world into "advanced" and "emerging" economies (based on per capita income level, export diversification[13] and the degree of integration into the global financial system[14]). The United Nations Conference on Trade and Development (UNCTAD) classifies countries into developed, transition and developing economies.[15] The OECD applies a four-tier classification: affluent countries (high-income countries), converging (catching up with the 'affluent' group), struggling (to reach middle-income levels) and poor (suffering extreme poverty) (OECD, 2010a). The latter two classifications, particularly, could be useful alternatives when classifying countries with regard to international migration, as they include information on current economic performance.

---

11   In the case of perfect equality, the IHDI is equal to the HDI, but falls below the HDI when inequality rises. In this sense, the IHDI is the actual level of human development (taking into account inequality), while the HDI can be viewed as an index of the potential human development that could be achieved if there were no inequality (http://hdr.undp.org/en/statistics/ihdi/).

12   The Multidimensional Poverty Index (MPI), published for the first time in the 2010 *Human Development Report*, complements money-based measures by considering multiple deprivations and their overlap. The index identifies deprivations across the same three dimensions as the HDI and shows the number of people who are multidimensionally poor (suffering deprivations in 33% of weighted indicators) and the number of deprivations with which poor households typically contend. It can be deconstructed by region, ethnicity and other groupings, as well as by dimension, making it an apt tool for policymakers (http://hdr.undp.org/en/statistics/mpi/).

13   This criterion prevents oil exporters with high per capita GDP from being included in the advanced classification because around 70 per cent of their exports are oil.

14   In the IMF classification, country grouping is more stable, over time, compared to the one used by the World Bank and UNDP. Indeed, given the volatility of per capita income levels and export diversifications, IMF uses an average over a number of years. Reclassification mainly takes place in the event of a more durable change (for example, Malta joining the European Union in 2008).

15   http://unctadstat.unctad.org/UnctadStatMetadata/Classifications/Methodology&Classifications.html.

Classifications used in this report

This report explores how migration trends vary, according to which definition of North or South is used.

- Chapter 2 uses all three definitions for the majority of analyses and shows how migration trends may vary according to which definition of North and South is used.

- Chapter 4, based on Gallup data, uses the classification proposed by the World Bank, which defines 'North' as high-income countries and 'South' as low-/middle-income countries. The World Bank definition was chosen because one of the most inherent characteristics of human mobility is the search for better job opportunities. Labour migration has remained the main driver throughout the history of international migration. Consequently, the majority of migrants move to countries with higher wage differentials – namely, countries with higher per capita incomes.[16]

Limitations and provisos

For a clear understanding of the analysis of, and findings on, the four migration pathways presented in this report, the following points should be borne in mind:

- Firstly, while the report tries to highlight common characteristics in each of the four pathways, there are relevant differences within each of them that will be referenced, to some extent.

- Secondly, while each of the four migration flows will be described as a stand-alone scenario, it is clear that they all form part of the global migration system and are closely interlinked (for example, restrictive migration policies in the North can lead to increased irregular South–North flows but also to an increase of South–South movements). While describing the key characteristics of each of the four migration flows separately, the report also highlights some of their possible interrelationships.

- Lastly, the description of the four migration flows in chapter 2 represents a snapshot of the situation in 2010. As the World Bank and UNDP reclassify countries on an annual basis, the composition of 'North' and 'South' changes too. Comparing 2010 figures with data from 1990 and 2000 would require adjusting the list of countries and would consequently bias the analysis.

Report structure

- Chapter 2 examines the current global migration situation, comparing patterns and characteristics of migratory movements, demographics, type of migration, and remittances across the four migration pathways: North–North, North–South, South–North, and South–South.

---

16 Migrants moving between developing countries seem to be even more attracted by the possibility of getting a job rather than by high wage differentials (Gagnon, J. and D. Khoudour-Castéras, 2011). Thus, emerging economies recording high growth rates might be more attractive than high-income but stagnant economies (also see box 2).

- Chapter 3 reviews existing research on the emerging field of happiness and subjective well-being, highlighting the importance of including subjective measures in assessments of well-being and evaluations of the impact of development on human lives. The chapter focuses on the connections between migration, income gains and happiness.

- Chapter 4 presents original findings on migrant well-being, from the Gallup World Poll, looking at outcomes for six core dimensions of well-being, across the four migration pathways.

- Chapter 5 draws conclusions and makes recommendations for future initiatives to monitor migrant well-being and the impact of migration on development, with reference to the inclusion of migration as a core issue in the post-2015 global development framework.

CONCLUDING REMARKS

For many years, policymakers have sought to unravel and better understand the connections between migration and development. This report presents a unique opportunity to look at the issue from a fresh perspective. In the Gallup Poll, migrants were asked whether they saw positive developments in their own lives. This, in turn, helped indicate what types of migration movements and experiences were likely to boost the development of economies and societies back home. The next chapter sets the scene for the interpretation of these original findings, showing how migration patterns can vary according to type of pathway and how 'South' and 'North' are defined.

 Migrant Voices

Providing for the family at home: Two Sri Lankan women working in Kuwait (South–North)

Dilini, security guard

Dilini, a 30-year-old woman from Sri Lanka who has been working in Kuwait for the past 13 years, left her home country desperate for work. "I am like many who lost their houses because of clashes going on," she says. Her eldest brother, a police officer, was injured in the fighting and couldn't work. Her father was too old and her sister too young to have regular employment. "The choice left to me was to try to find oversees work as a housemaid somewhere in the Gulf Cooperation Countries, if this family wanted to survive and have another house to live in," she explains. She was initially reticent about becoming a security guard – a position that is still not customary for women in Kuwait. "Being a security guard was a little embarrassing for me, at the beginning," she says, "but compared to the job that I had been doing for 10 years as a housemaid, my current position is much better for my privacy, working hours and income."

Yet the reality in Kuwait did not live up to Dilini's hopes: "Work agencies describe living abroad as a heaven of money, but this was not what I found when I arrived in Kuwait," she said. "I had to work for so many hours to earn USD100 every month" – to have enough money to send back home. Tragedy struck in Sri Lanka with the 2005 tsunami, and Dilini was forced to prolong her stay beyond the initial two-year contract: "The house that I built to accommodate my family away from the Tamil clashes was destroyed, but this time by a tsunami," she says. "I kept saying 'one more year then I will go back home', but things didn't work out that way." But she also has "big worries" about no longer fitting in back home. The kind of life she has in Kuwait would not be affordable in Sri Lanka: "I even feel my mentality now is not at all like when I was at home." She fears that she will grow old without ever getting married: "When I am done in Kuwait, will a loving husband be difficult for me to find?"

Shirmila, domestic help

"I didn't choose to work abroad but, like many in the village, due to little income and the clashes going on between the Tamils and the government, I had to try the agencies that were sending people abroad for a better income," says Shirmila, a Sri Lankan woman now working as a domestic helper in Kuwait. The travel process was smooth and the biggest challenges were the language barriers and missing her husband back home. "I was very lucky and worked for a lovely family," she said. "They helped me a lot to make things easier."

Shirmila had a terrible shock when visiting home for the first time after seven years away.

As she recounts: "I knocked on the door of my dream house – the house that I was building by sending my husband every dollar I could save in Kuwait – and a strange woman opened the door and said she was my husband's wife! My first thought was: 'I wish I hadn't travelled or had the working abroad contract; I've lost everything'." However, now she is thankful for her decision to return to Kuwait: "Thank God I decided to come back to Kuwait and not to give up just because of the house and the husband that I lost."

After 24 years, she is still in Kuwait and has managed to bring her children over to join her and to find them good jobs. "They are around me all the time," she says, "and we enjoy being together on weekends with many other community members." Moreover, she has managed to build a house back in Sri Lanka and to ensure that her grandchildren have a good standard of living.

Chapter 2

Migration trends: Comparing the four pathways

Rudolf Anich, Tara Brian and Frank Laczko

HIGHLIGHTS

Most migration is to countries in the North but it is almost matched by migration to countries in the South[17] – an overlooked and likely underestimated phenomenon, given the difficulty in finding reliable statistics.

Most migrants are from countries in the South, in absolute terms, because the collective population of those nations is higher. Relatively speaking, however, people from countries in the North are more likely to migrate.

For each of the four migration pathways, the top migration corridors are:

- North–North: Germany to the United States, followed by the United Kingdom to Australia, and then Canada, the Republic of Korea and the United Kingdom to the United States.

- South–South: Ukraine to the Russian Federation, followed by the Russian Federation to Ukraine, Bangladesh to Bhutan, and Kazakhstan to the Russian Federation and Afghanistan.

- South–North: Mexico to the United States, followed by Turkey to Germany, and then China, the Philippines and India to the United States.

- North–South: the United States to Mexico and South Africa, followed by Germany to Turkey, Portugal to Brazil, and Italy to Argentina.

More than half of the top 20 migration corridors worldwide are accounted for by people migrating from South to South.

The majority of migrants are male, except in the case of North–North migration.

Migrants in the South are younger than migrants in the North.

Most international students go to the North to study.

Most of the money migrants send home ('remittances') goes from North to South, although there are significant flows between countries of the South.

Migration by people from North to South is an increasingly important but neglected trend. Such moves are prompted by a variety of motives – for instance, to explore economic opportunities in the global market place, to study or retire abroad, or (among the diaspora) to re-connect with their country of origin.

17 The report adopts the terminology used in development discourse to categorize countries according to their economic status. This matter is discussed in detail in chapter 1 but, broadly speaking, 'North' refers to high-income countries and 'South' to low- and middle-income countries.

This chapter has two main objectives:

1. ***To present international migration and development trends from a different perspective, by presenting data according to the four pathways of movement: North–North, North–South, South–South and South–North.*** *Typically, in debates about migration and development, the focus is on trends in South–North migration (for instance, a nurse moving from Turkey to Germany) and, to some extent, South–South migration (for example, a builder who moves from the Ukraine to the Russian Federation). In this report, it is argued that when a migrant moves from North to North (for example, a nurse going from Australia to the United Kingdom), or from North to South (such as when a young engineer goes from the United States to South Africa in search of work), there are also implications for development. This chapter provides an important context for the discussion in chapter 4, by showing how the profile of migrants and the scale and direction of movements vary according to the four pathways.*

2. ***To explore how these trends vary according to which definition of 'South' and 'North' is used.*** *As discussed in chapter 1, the report compares data using the three main ways of defining North and South, as adopted by UN DESA, the World Bank and UNDP. Figures on international migration in the North and the South differ according to the definition used. Some countries may be part of the 'North', in one classification, while being grouped into the 'South' in another categorization. Key borderline countries include the Russian Federation and transition economies in Eastern Europe, some Gulf Cooperation Council (GCC) countries (such as Bahrain, Qatar and the United Arab Emirates), some of the emerging Asian economies (such as Hong Kong, China; the Republic of Korea; and Singapore) and Caribbean countries (such as Barbados; Bermuda; Puerto Rico; and Trinidad and Tobago).*

This chapter will provide a snapshot of the situation at a particular point in time (2010), rather than an analysis over time, since countries are reclassified annually under most indexing systems[18] and the composition of 'North' and 'South' therefore changes every year. In addition, definitions or methodologies used by these systems may also vary, making it impossible to make an accurate longitudinal comparison. This chapter therefore provides key migration statistics for each of the four migratory pathways in 2010.

---

18 UNDP and the World Bank do an annual reclassification of countries in terms of the HDI and GNI per capita. These adjustments give a more accurate reflection of the current status of development, but it means that figures are not easily comparable, over time. Instead, UN DESA's definition is not linked to an index or indicator that is regularly updated. Countries defined as part of the North or South have remained roughly the same over the last few decades. This means that the data can be directly compared, but the classification system can result in a given country still being designated as 'North' or 'South', even if its development status has significantly changed, over time.

Four migration pathways

South–North and South–South represent the two major migratory flows in all three classification systems (see figure 1 and table 2).

- According to the classification used by the World Bank, in 2010, South–North movements represented the largest migratory flow (45% of the total), followed by South–South (35%), North–North (17%) and North–South (3%) (see table 2).

 Table 2   Stock of international migrants (in thousands) and share of global migrant stock on the four migration pathways, using the three key classifications, 2010

	S–N		N–N		S–S		N–S	
	Stock (thousand)	%	Stock (thousand)	%	Stock (thousand)	%	Stock (thousand)	%
UN DESA	74,297	35	53,464	25	73,158	34	13,279	6
WB	95,091	45	36,710	17	75,355	35	7,044	3
UNDP	86,873	41	32,757	15	87,159	41	7,410	3

Source: IOM calculations, based on UN DESA, 2012b.

 Figure 1   Stock of international migrants (in millions), on the four migration pathways, using the three key classifications, 2010

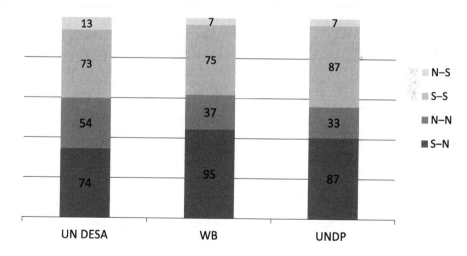

Source: IOM calculations, based on UN DESA, 2012b.

The difference between the classifications used becomes more relevant when considering both the origin and the destination of international migrants along the four pathways of migration.

- For instance, for North–North migration, UN DESA values are almost twice as high as the ones obtained when using the UNDP definition (for example, 25% and 15%, respectively, in terms of the share of the global migrant stock).

- The scale of North–South migration varies from a high of 13 million, using UN DESA figures, to 7 million, according to the UNDP and World Bank definitions.

- The figures for South–South migrants also vary significantly – from 87 million, according to UNDP figures, to 75 and 73 million, respectively, according to the World Bank and UN DESA definitions.

- As for South–North migration, the World Bank counts 95 million persons moving in this direction, compared to 87 million, according to UNDP, and 74 million, for UN DESA.

- The majority of migrants live in the North, according to all three definitions, with values ranging between 56 and 62 per cent (see table 3).[19]

 Table 3   Stock of international migrants (in thousands) and share of global migrant stock living in the North and South, using the three key classifications, 2010

	To North		To South	
	Stock (thousand)	%	Stock (thousand)	%
UN DESA	127,762	60	86,438	40
WB	131,800	62	82,399	38
UNDP	119,630	56	94,569	44

Source: IOM calculations, based on UN DESA, 2012b.

South–North migration increased the most in the last two decades.

- Looking at how migrant numbers have changed, over time, it is likely that South–North migration will play an increasing role (UNGA, 2012), although South–South migration flows, which are much more likely to be under-recorded, could possibly be the dominant pathway or, at least, be as important as the South–North flows.

- While North–South migration has remained stable, over the past 20 years, and South–South and North–North migration have increased by less than one third, South–North migration appears to have doubled in that time (see figure 2).

- However, it is important to remember that, in the South–South context, informal movements are likely to be more common and, therefore, unrecorded movements not reflected in the figures below are likely to be much higher. Data-gathering capacities in the South are also much more limited.

19 As a comparison, the extended version of the Database on Immigrants in OECD Countries (DIOC-E - version 2.0, which includes 89 destination countries, 61 of which are outside the OECD area covering 72% of global migrants) recorded 68 per cent of all migrants living in the North (i.e. OECD countries) and 32 per cent living in the South (i.e. non-OECD countries) (Dumont et al., 2010).

Figure 2   Evolution of migrant stocks (in millions) on the four migration pathways, according to the three key classifications, 1990–2010

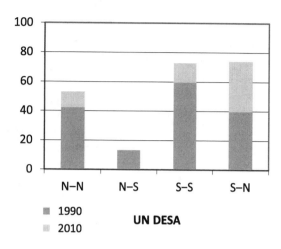

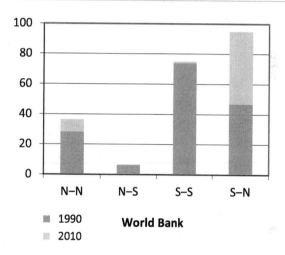

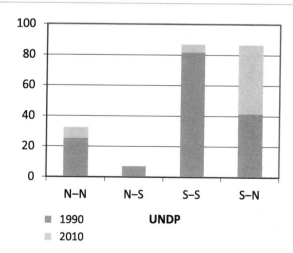

Source: IOM calculations, based on UN DESA, 2012b.

Note: Calculations were made by keeping country classifications stable (i.e. 2010 classifications were also used for 1990 figures). However, using the World Bank's 1990 classification revealed the same trends, with South–South migration even decreasing in the 1990–2010 period. The UN DESA classification hardly changed while, for UNDP, no 'very high HDI' category was available in 1990.

Migrant origin

In absolute terms, the majority of international migrants originate in the South, which is not surprising, given the much larger population in the South than in the North.

- Indeed, values range between 147 and 174 million migrants (equal to 69% and 81%, respectively, of the global migrant stock) born in developing countries (see table 4).

- In other words, three out of four migrants are likely to come from the South, according to the classification used by the World Bank and UNDP, and two out of three, using the UN DESA classification.

 Table 4 Stock of international migrants (in thousands) and share of global migrant stock originating in the North and South, using the three key classifications, 2010

	From North		From South	
	Stock (thousand)	%	Stock (thousand)	%
UN DESA	66,744	31	147,456	69
WB	43,753	20	170,446	80
UNDP	40,167	19	174,032	81

Source: IOM calculations, based on UN DESA, 2012b.

However, in relative terms, people originating in the North are more likely to migrate than those in the South.

- This is important, in the context of the migration–development debate. Migration is usually considered to be prompted by the search for a better life by people in poorer countries, with the lack of development in these countries being a key 'push factor'. The assumption is that, if development increased, migration would decrease. In fact, people who are already living in a more developed country may be as likely to migrate as those living in developing countries.

- De Haas (2010) found an inverted-U-shape relationship between the level of human development and migration patterns, indicating that the number of people leaving a country only starts declining once a high level of human development has been reached in the country of origin. This means that the number of migrants continues to rise, even when there's an increase in the level of human development, and that countries with high human development levels can have as many people leaving as can countries with low levels.

- When comparing the total number of migrants with the total population residing in the South and North, respectively, the role of human mobility in the North becomes more evident. While the absolute number of migrants is higher for the South, people living in the North are more mobile and, therefore, represent a higher share of the total population living there.

- In fact, according to all three classifications, in the North, emigrants represent a higher percentage of the total population (between 3.6% and 5.2%) than they do in the South (less than 3%) (see table 5 below).

- In other words, the total number of migrants originating in the South is higher than in the North, but migrants account for a smaller percentage, if compared to the population living in the South and the North, respectively.

Migrant destination

An assessment of international migration along all four migration pathways reveals the significance of the South as a destination for migrants.

- It highlights the importance of South–South movements and reminds us that a significant number of people (between 7 million and 13 million) also move from the North to the South and, indeed, there are several indications that this trend has been increasing (see later in this chapter for more details).

- However, when comparing the number of immigrants with the total population living in the South and the North, the picture changes. For all classifications, international migrants in the South represent less than 2 per cent of the total population; in the North, they range between 10 and 12 per cent (see table 5). This difference can partially be explained by the demographic boom in many developing countries and the decline of birth rates in more developed countries, over the last few decades.

 Table 5 Immigrants and emigrants as a share of the total population in the North and South, using the three key classifications, 2010

	North			South		
	Population (million)	Immigrants (as % of pop)	Emigrants (as % of pop)	Population (million)	Immigrants (as % of pop)	Emigrants (as % of pop)
UN DESA	1,237	11.3	5.2	5,671	1.52	2.5
WB	1,100	12.0	3.8	5,807	1.41	2.9
UNDP	1,056	10.3	3.6	5,852	1.61	2.9

Source: IOM calculations, based on UN DESA, 2011a and 2012b.

World's top migration corridors

More than half the top 20 migration corridors worldwide (that is, those with the highest number of migrants moving between two countries) are along the South–South pathway, and the United States is the top destination for migrants from both the North and the South (see map 2).

- South–South corridors include, primarily, migrants moving from the Russian Federation to the Ukraine and Kazakhstan, and vice versa. Other major corridors are Bangladesh to India; Afghanistan to Pakistan and Iran; and India to Pakistan, and vice versa; and Indonesia to Malaysia.

- The only corridor from the African continent in the top 20 is from Burkina Faso to Côte d'Ivoire.

- The United States represents the key destination for major migrant corridors in the North–North and South–North context (see table 6). Migrants moving from Mexico to the United States rank first, totalling alone almost 6 per cent of the global migrant stock. Other major countries of origin include China, India and the Philippines, in the South, and Canada, Germany and the Republic of Korea, in the North.

- There is also a significant number of nationals moving from the United Kingdom to Australia.

- None of the top 20 corridors runs from the North to the South. However, significant numbers of migrants have been recorded along this pathway, with US nationals moving to Mexico and, more surprisingly, to South Africa; Germans moving to Turkey; and Portuguese moving to Brazil. Some of these movements are due to retirement and rising unemployment in the North, among others (as discussed later in this chapter).

Map 2 Top 20 migration corridors worldwide (migrant stock, in thousands), using the World Bank classification, 2010

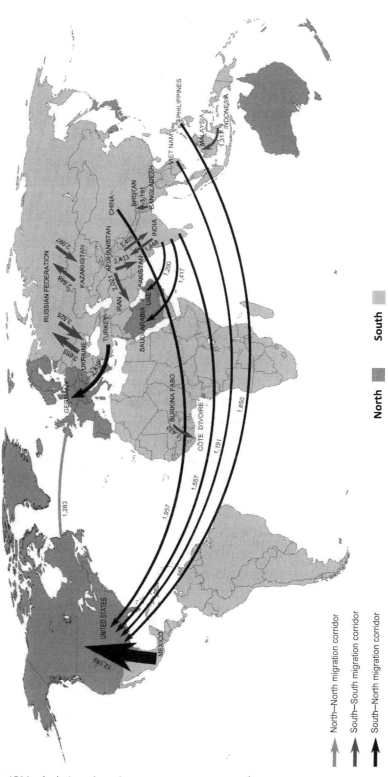

Source: IOM calculations, based on UN DESA, 2012b.

Notes: 1) The boundaries and names shown and the designations used on this map do not imply official endorsement or acceptance by the International Organization for Migration (IOM). Dotted lines are used to indicate administrative boundaries, undetermined boundaries and situations where the final boundary has not yet been determined.

2) Four migration corridors are excluded from this ranking: China to Hong Kong, China (ranking eighth); movements within the Occupied Palestinian Territory (eleventh); Occupied Palestinian Territory to Jordan (thirteenth); and Puerto Rico to the United States (fourteenth).

Table 6   Top five migrant corridors on each of the four migration pathways, using the World Bank classification, 2010

S–N	Origin	Destination	Number of migrants	% of total S–N migrants
1	Mexico	United States	12,189,158	12.8
2	Turkey	Germany	2,819,326	3.0
3	China	United States	1,956,523	2.1
4	Philippines	United States	1,850,067	1.9
5	India	United States	1,556,641	0.7
N–N	**Origin**	**Destination**	**Number of migrants**	**% of total N–N migrants**
1	Germany	United States	1,283,108	4.0
2	United Kingdom	Australia	1,097,893	3.5
3	Canada	United States	1,037,187	3.0
4	Korea, Republic of	United States	1,030,561	2.8
5	United Kingdom	United States	901,916	2.5
S–S	**Origin**	**Destination**	**Number of migrants**	**% of total S–S migrants**
1	Ukraine	Russian Federation	3,662,722	4.9
2	Russian Federation	Ukraine	3,524,669	4.7
3	Bangladesh	India	3,190,769	4.2
4	Kazakhstan	Russian Federation	2,648,316	3.5
5	Afghanistan	Pakistan	2,413,395	3.2
N–S	**Origin**	**Destination**	**Number of migrants**	**% of total N–S migrants**
1	United States	Mexico	563,315	7.8
2	Germany	Turkey	306,459	4.3
3	United States	South Africa	252,311	3.5
4	Portugal	Brazil	222,148	3.1
5	Italy	Argentina	198,319	2.8

Source: IOM calculations, based on UN DESA, 2012b.
Note: Two migratory flows are excluded from this ranking: China to Hong Kong, China (ranking third in South–North) and movements from Puerto Rico to the United States (first in North–North).

Main migrant-sending and -receiving countries

The top migrant-sending and -receiving countries in the world are the United States, the Russian Federation, Ukraine and India, but there are other notable trends also (see figure 3 and map 2).

- EU Member States, such as Germany, Italy, Poland and the United Kingdom, are the major countries of origin in the North–North context.

- The United States attracts many other nationalities (from Canada, China, Mexico, Puerto Rico, the Philippines and the Republic of Korea), representing the major destination for both South–North and North–North migration (receiving, respectively, 35% and 27% of all migrants in each of the two migratory flows).

- The United States is also the major migrant-sending country for North–South migration (particularly to Mexico and South Africa).

- For South–South migratory flows, countries such as the Russian Federation, Ukraine and India are both major sending and receiving countries.

- Major South–South sending countries include several Asian countries, such as Afghanistan and Bangladesh, and receiving countries include Kazakhstan and Pakistan.

In terms of migrants as a share of the total population, countries with a smaller total population tend to rank highest.

- Findings worth noting are the high shares of immigrants in the population of destination countries in the South–North context – in particular, in some of the Gulf Cooperation Council (GCC) countries (86% for Qatar, 68% for United Arab Emirates, and 66% for Kuwait).

- Interestingly, many countries where emigrants represent a particularly high share of the total population are part of the North–North world. In some high-income Caribbean countries, such as Barbados, for example, emigrants moving to another country in the North represent 39 per cent of the total population; in Puerto Rico and Trinidad and Tobago, they represent 37 per cent and 25 per cent, respectively; and, in some EU Member States, they also account for a significant share (Malta 23%, Portugal 18%, Croatia and Ireland 15%).

Figure 3   Top five countries of destination and origin, on the four migration pathways (migrants in thousands and as share of total migrant stock, on each pathway), using the World Bank classification, 2010

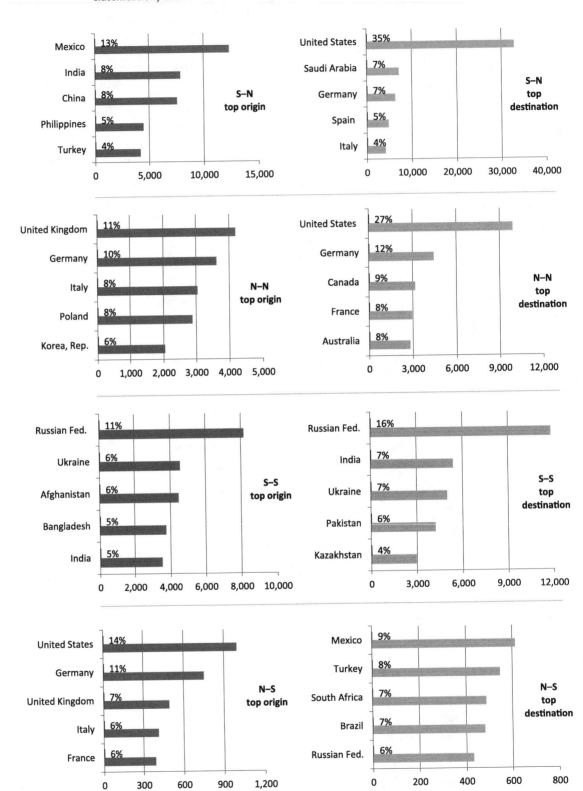

Source: IOM calculations, based on UN DESA, 2012b.
Note: Not included in this figure: in the South–South 'top origin' category, Occupied Palestinian Territory, which ranks second in the South–South 'top destination' category, Jordan, which ranks fifth and mainly receives migrants from the Occupied Palestinian Territory.

Migration and gender

The majority of migrants are male, except in the case of North–North migration, where the majority are female.

- Female migrants, when calculated as a share of the total migrant population for each of the four migration pathways, were found to be in the majority only in the North–North context. This was consistently found to be the case, regardless of which classification was used (see figure 4).

- In all other migratory flows, female migrants are fewer in number than men (with the exception of female migrants moving North–South, if using the UN DESA classification, and South–South, according to the World Bank classification).

- In line with figures on the overall migrant stock, the greatest share of female migrants were likely to move from the South to the North and only slightly fewer within the South (see figure 5).

- About 60 per cent of all female migrants live, like their male counterparts, in the North and about 10 per cent of them are international migrants.

Figure 4 Female migrants as a share of the total migrant stock on the four migration pathways, using the three key classifications, 2010

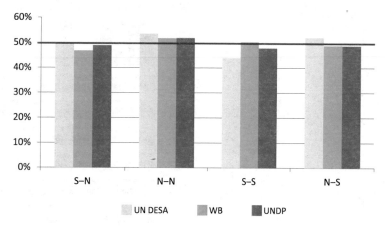

Source: IOM calculations, based on UN DESA, 2012b.

Figure 5 Female migrants as a share of the total female migrant stock on the four migration pathways, using the three key classifications, 2010

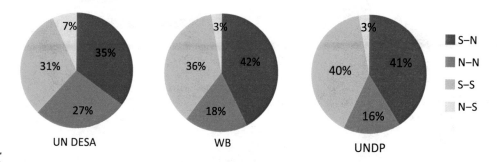

Source: IOM calculations, based on UN DESA, 2012b.

Migration and age

International migrants in the South are, on average, younger than those in the North.

- The percentage of migrants of up to 24 years of age is much higher in the South than in the North (see figure 6).

- Migrants in the North have a stronger presence in the working-age groups (especially among 25–49-year-olds), which becomes particularly clear when comparing migrants with the total population (see figure 7).

- Finally, in the South, migrants have been found to represent a higher share of the older age groups, compared to nationals (see figure 7). This holds true particularly for female migrants – possibly due to good living standards, which persuade migrants to stay, or some sort of difficulty returning home. It might also partially reflect the increasing retirement migration from North to South (see end of this chapter for more details).

Figure 6 Migrants by age group and gender in the North and the South, using the World Bank classification, 2010

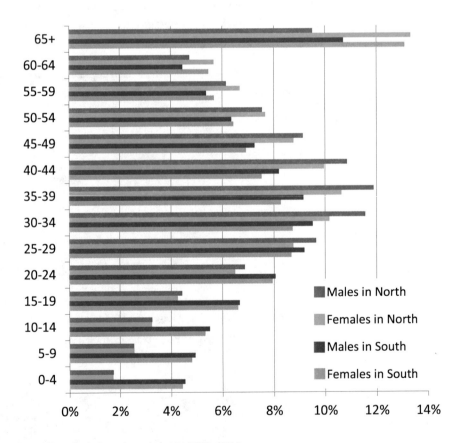

Source: IOM calculations, based on UN DESA, 2011a.

Figure 7   Total population and migrants by age group in the North and the South, according to the
World Bank classification, 2010

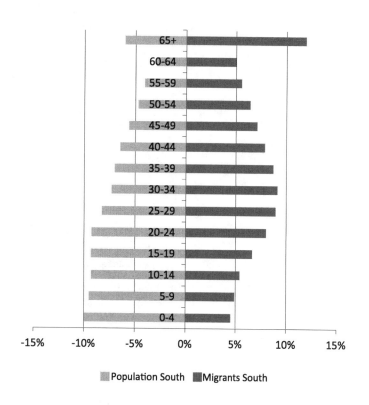

Population South   Migrants South

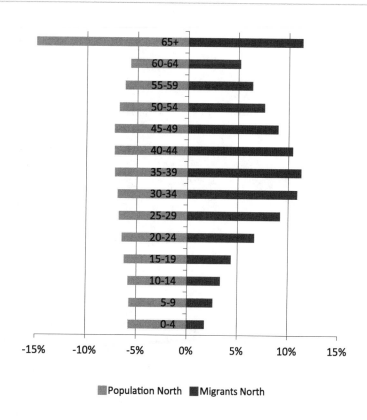

Population North   Migrants North

Source: IOM calculations, based on UN DESA, 2011a.
Note: Data exclude countries or areas with fewer than 100,000 inhabitants in 2010, due to lack
of disaggregated data.

Migration and work skills

Migrants are predominantly low-skilled, although reliable up-to-date information is largely missing, particularly for countries in the South.

- From the data collected by the DIOC-E,[20] it appears that migration remains predominantly low-skilled, both in the North and in the South:[21] 44 per cent of migrants are low-skilled, 33 per cent have intermediate skills; and only 22 per cent are highly skilled (Dumont et al., 2010).

- Migration by low-skilled workers is likely to play a greater role in the South–South context, which is characterized by informal, less costly movements to neighbouring countries and is therefore accessible to larger and less educated parts of the population (GFMD, 2012).

- In all world regions, tertiary emigration rates[22] are higher than the total emigration rate in all world regions.[23] OECD estimates highlight that, in the North, 24 per cent of all migrants have completed tertiary education, while only 15 per cent of migrants in the South have reached this level of education (Dumont et al., 2010).[24] However, attractive destinations for highly skilled migrants also exist in the South – for instance, in some of the Gulf Cooperation Council (GCC) countries, Malaysia and South Africa (GFMD, 2012).

Refugees

Contrary to public perception, the majority of refugees not only originate but also live in the South.

- In 2010, using the World Bank classification, four out of five refugees were born and were living in the South (accounting for 81% of the global number of refugees).

- The North hosts fewer than one in five refugees but also generates a much more limited number of refugees (less than 1% of the global stock) (see table 7). Most of them are Croatians living in other States of the former Yugoslavia – most notably, Serbia.

- These findings are confirmed when refugees are considered as a share of the total migrant stock in each of the four migration pathways: only in the South–South context do refugees make up a significant proportion of migrants – that is, more than 10 per cent of all migrants.

---

20 The extended version of the Database on Immigrants in OECD Countries (DIOC-E, version 2.0) covers 89 destination countries (61 of which are outside the OECD area) and includes about 110 million migrants.

21 North and South are here defined as OECD and non-OECD countries, respectively, and not according to the World Bank classification used before in this part.

22 The stock of emigrants from a given country having (at least) completed a higher education degree (13 years or more) expressed as a share of the total labour force with tertiary education in that country.

23 This is particularly true for Africa, where the emigration rate of highly skilled migrants (10.6% globally and 9.7% to OECD countries) is double that estimated for other regions (5.4% and 4.3%, respectively) (Dumont et al., 2010).

24 North and South are here defined as OECD and non-OECD countries, respectively, and not according to the World Bank classification previously used in this section.

Table 7   Number of refugees (in thousands), share of global refugee stock and share of migrant stock in each of the four migration pathways, using the World Bank classification, 2010

	S–N	N–N	S–S	N–S
Stock (in thousands)	1,756	19	7,939	61
% of global refugee stock	18%	0.2%	81.2%	0.6%
% of total migrants (in each pathway)	1.8%	0.1%	10.5%	0.9%

Source: Own calculations, based on UNHCR Statistical Online Population Database.

Note: Data do not include stateless persons (estimated at up to 12 million, as of end of 2010),Palestinian refugees residing in areas of the United Nations Relief and Works Agency for Palestinian Refugees in the Near East (UNRWA)(4.8 million), and people in refugee-like situations (about 775,000). For details, see www.unhcr.org/pages/49c3646c4d6.html.

International students

Most international students go to educational institutions in the North.[25]

- In the academic year 2009/2010, four out of five international students[26] were living in the North, using the World Bank classification.

- Today, more than half of all international students originate in the South and study in the North (see table 8). Almost one third are North–North students, mainly because of the opportunities to study in Europe, such as the EU Erasmus Programme.[27]

- The figure for South–South students is significantly lower (only 18%), despite the fact that South–South migrants account for 35 per cent of the global migrant stock.

- Educational opportunities in the North may, indeed, be more attractive, due to higher quality, prestige and reputation, and the greater availability of part-time jobs. However, regional hubs for pursuing studies also exist in the South – for instance, more than half of the international students originating in countries belonging to the Southern African Development Community (SADC) decide to study within the region and, more precisely, in South Africa. SADC countries ranked first, globally, in terms of outbound mobility ratio of tertiary students (UNESCO, 2012).[28]

---

25   Calculations are based on available bilateral country data on international student mobility, which are not available for all student migrants. The *Global Education Digest 2011*, prepared by the United Nations Educational, Scientific and Cultural Organization (UNESCO), reports a total number of 3,369,244 internal mobile students for 2009/2010; however, this is not disaggregated according to origin and destination country. A detailed breakdown by country of origin is available in the online database of the UNESCO Institute for Statistics (UIS) but it includes only about one third of the global stock of international mobile students (i.e. slightly more than 1 million). Thus, these calculations represent only a rough approximation of the total distribution of students between the four pathways of migration, as defined by the *WMR 2013*. For more information, see: www.uis.unesco.org/Pages/default.aspx and www.uis.unesco.org/Education/Pages/ged-2011.aspx.

26   The UIS defines internationally mobile students as those who study in a foreign country, of which they are not a permanent resident (UNESCO, 2009).

27   In 2009/2010, the number of Erasmus students alone exceeded 200,000; see: http://ec.europa.eu/education/pub/pdf/higher/erasmus0910_en.pdf.

28   The number of students from a given country studying abroad, expressed as a share of the total tertiary enrolment in the country.

- Finally, it should be noted that these data on bilateral flows do not capture the entire global mobile student population (see footnote 25) and data on students in the South may be under-recorded.

 Table 8   Stock of international students (in thousands) on each of the four migration pathways, using the World Bank classification, 2009/2010

	S–N	N–N	S–S	N–S
Stock of international students	535,694	297,102	191,739	17,031
% of global student stock	51%	29%	18%	2%

Source: IOM calculations, based on United Nations Educational, Scientific and Cultural Organization (UNESCO) Institute of Statistics (UIS) data, extracted in September 2012.

Note: Figures included in this calculation only represent about one third of the total number of international mobile students and, thus, are only an approximation of the total distribution between the four pathways of migration.

Key remittance patterns

Officially recorded remittance flows show that the largest share of remittance transfers are from North to South, but flows between countries in the South are also important; two thirds of remittances received by the least developed countries (LDCs)[29] originate in the South (UNCTAD, 2012).

- This is in keeping with data showing that most movements are from South to North and, therefore, most remittances are sent from the North to the South: in 2010, these movements accounted for almost two thirds of the total remittances (USD 267 billion), using the World Bank classification, more than half of the total (USD 242 billion), using the UNDP classification, and more than 40 per cent (USD 185 billion), using the UN DESA classification (see figure 8).

- This is also the result of higher wage differentials in the South–North context and higher transfer costs between countries in the South.

- But it is also estimated that the amount of remittances transferred through informal, unrecorded channels is particularly high in the South–South context (Ratha and Shaw, 2010).

- Using the World Bank classification, the share of South–South remittances is particularly low as transfers from high-income countries in the southern hemisphere (such as from countries in the GCC to Asia) are not included.

29   LDCs are defined by the Economic and Social Council of the United Nations on the basis of three criteria: low income, human resource weakness and economic vulnerability. See web link for further details: www.un.org/special-rep/ohrlls/ldc/ldc%20criteria.htm.

Figure 8   Comparing remittance flows (in USD billions) on the four migration pathways

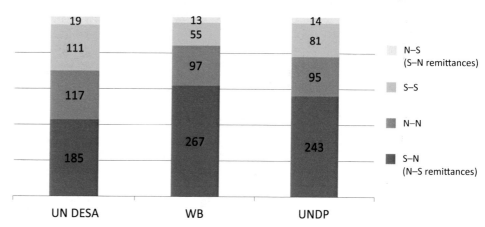

Source: IOM calculations, based on World Bank, 2010.
Notes: 1) The following countries and territories are excluded, due to lack of data: Aruba; French Polynesia; Macao, China; Netherlands Antilles; New Caledonia; West Bank and Gaza.
2) Due to the lack of disaggregated data, UN DESA figures include Saint Pierre and Miquelon as part of the South, although classified by UN DESA as being in the North.

South–North migrants remit proportionately more than migrants on the other three pathways.

- According to all three key classifications, while South–North migrants represent 35–45 per cent of all migrants, they send between 43 and 62 per cent of all remittances. The same phenomenon can be observed for North–North migrants, although to a lesser extent (see table 9).

- These figures indicate that migrants living in the North send more remittances than their counterparts in the South. This is particularly so if compared with South–South migrants, who represent more than one third of the global migrant stock but remit only a quarter of all remittances or less.

- Interestingly, these results are different when considering only remittances to LDCs, two thirds of which, according to the United Nations Conference on Trade and Development (UNCTAD, 2012), originate in countries in the South. This can be explained by the fact that migrants from LDCs mainly move to other developing countries and only one out of four migrates to a developed country.[30]

- As mentioned above, these results can be partly explained by differences in the transfer costs, wage differentials and unrecorded remittance flows.

30 For more information, see http://unctad.org/en/docs/ldc2011_en.pdf.

Table 9   Comparison of migrant stocks and remittance levels on the four pathways, using the three key classifications, 2010

		S–N (N–S remittances)	N–N	S–S	N–S (S–N remittances)
UN DESA	**Migrants as %** of global migrant stock	35%	25%	34%	6%
	% of global **remittances**	43%	27%	26%	4%
WB	**Migrants as %** of global migrant stock	45%	17%	35%	3%
	% of global **remittances**	62%	22%	13%	3%
UNDP	**Migrants as %** of global migrant stock	41%	15%	41%	3%
	% of global **remittances**	56%	22%	19%	3%

Source: IOM calculations, based on World Bank, 2010.

Notes: 1) The following countries and territories are excluded, due to lack of data: Aruba; French Polynesia; Macao, China; Netherlands Antilles; New Caledonia; West Bank and Gaza.

2) Due to the lack of disaggregated data, UN DESA figures include Saint Pierre and Miquelon as part of the South, although classified by UN DESA as being in the North.

World's top remittance corridors

Key notable points about the top remittance corridors (those with the highest total number of transfers between two countries) are that the majority are part of the South–North migratory flow; the United States is the top remittance-sending country; and the top remittance-receiving countries are in Asia (see map 3).

- Out of the top 20 global remittance corridors, 16 are part of the South–North migratory flow.

- The only exceptions are remittances sent from India to Bangladesh (ranking twelfth), Malaysia to Indonesia (fourteenth), France to Belgium (nineteenth) and France to Spain (twentieth).

- The United States is the top remittance-sending country in four of the top five corridors. In 2010, almost USD 100 billion were sent from the United States to countries in the South, accounting for more than one third of all remittance flows in the South–North migration world.

- In the same year, the top five corridors each recorded more than USD 10 billion in remittances, led by the United States–Mexico (USD 22 billion) and the United Arab Emirates–India (USD 14 billion).

- In the North–North context, EU Member States are major remittance-receiving but also -sending countries. More than half of all North–North remittances are received by the top five receiving countries, which are all EU Member States. Remittances are sent from within the EU, from countries such as France and Spain, but also from outside, such as Australia and the United States (see also table 10 and figure 9).

- In the South–South context, remittances in four of the top five corridors are bi-directional (that is, they are transmitted and received between the same countries), reflecting the economic linkages between India and Bangladesh, and between the Russian Federation and Ukraine.

- As for the North–South migration pathway, the major corridors are closely linked with the top remittance-sending and -receiving corridors, highlighting the long-standing relations between countries – namely, Germany and Turkey; Spain and Argentina; and the United States and Mexico.

 Table 10   Top five remittance corridors on the four migration pathways (remittances in USD millions), using the World Bank classification, 2010

Rank	South–North (N–S remittances)	North–North	South–South	North–South (S–N remittances)
1	US → Mexico (22,190)	France → Belgium (3,148)	India → Bangladesh (3,769)	Turkey → Germany (994)
2	UAE → India (13,821)	France → Spain (2,743)	Malaysia → Indonesia (3,430)	Argentina → Spain (927)
3	US → China (12,205)	Spain → France (2,302)	Russian Fed. → Ukraine (2,720)	Mexico → USA (655)
4	US → India (11,977)	US → Germany (2,154)	Bangladesh → India (1,899)	Belarus → Poland (578)
5	US → Philippines (10,117)	Australia → UK (1,939)	Ukraine → Russian Fed. (1,788)	Kazakhstan → Germany (570)

Source: IOM calculations, based on World Bank, 2010.
Note: The remittance corridor Hong Kong, China to China (ranking third) has been excluded from this ranking.

Map 3 Top 20 remittance corridors worldwide (remittances in USD millions), using the World Bank classification, 2010

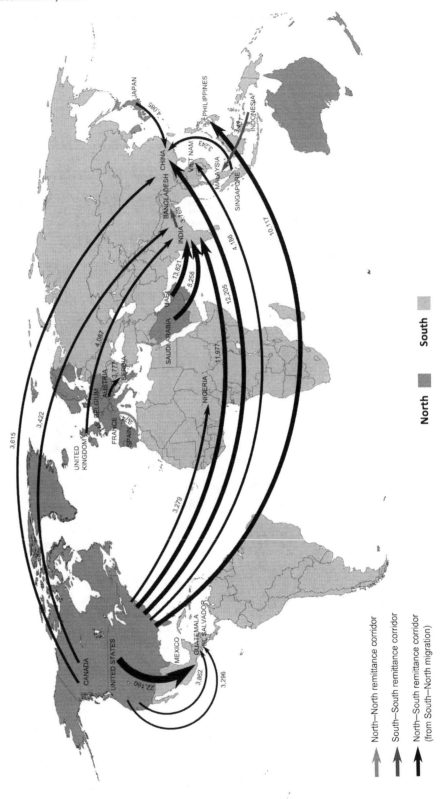

Source: IOM calculations, based on World Bank, 2010.

Notes: 1) The boundaries and names shown and the designations used on this map do not imply official endorsement or acceptance by the International Organization for Migration (IOM). Dotted lines are used to indicate administrative boundaries, undetermined boundaries and situations where the final boundary has not yet been determined.

2) The remittance corridor Hong Kong, China to China (ranking third) has been excluded from this ranking.

Figure 9   Top five countries sending and receiving remittances on the four migration pathways (remittances in millions USD and as a share of total remittances, on each pathway), using the World Bank classification, 2010

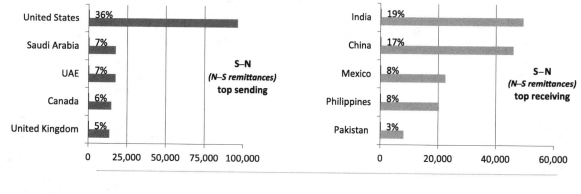

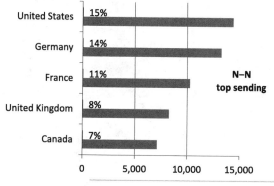

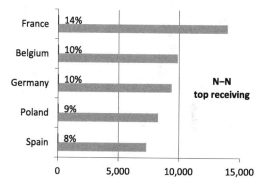

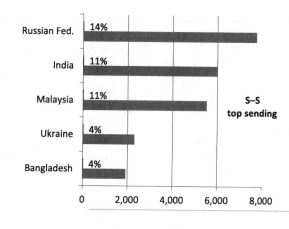

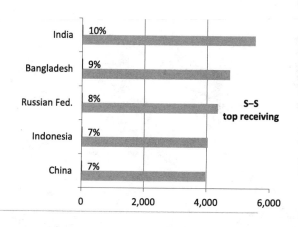

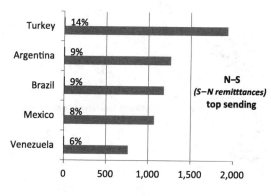

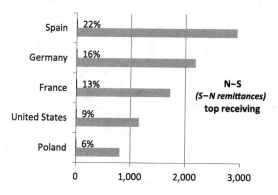

Source: IOM calculations, based on World Bank, 2010.

Note: On the South–South pathway, Jordan has been excluded from the ranking of top remittance-sending countries; it ranks fourth and mainly sends remittances to the Occupied Palestinian Territory.

IN FOCUS: NORTH–SOUTH MIGRATION

Trends

South–North migration accounts for less than half of all migratory flows globally but has tended to dominate policy discussions on migration and development. Migration from developed to developing regions, or from North to South, tends to be particularly neglected. Yet, although this flow accounts for just 3–6 per cent[31] of total migration, or between 7 and 13 million migrants, there is evidence that this flow is increasing. While it is too early to see changes in North–South migration reflected in global databases,[32] country-specific examples and anecdotal evidence suggest that this trend is becoming increasingly important. For example, China's stock of international migrants has risen by 35 per cent in the last 10 years, with an increasing number likely to originate in the North; the number of Portuguese migrants in Africa has increased by 42 per cent, over the past decade; and the United States has become the main country of origin for migrants heading to Brazil.

 Box 3

Migration to China

- Numbers of international migrants are increasing.

- There were 685,775 migrants in China in 2010 – up by 35 per cent since 2000. Numbers of foreigners holding permits also rose by around 29 per cent, compared with 2006 (OECD, 2012a).

- China is an increasingly attractive destination, due to its rapid economic growth and demographic changes. Labour market needs are outstripping supply (Skeldon, 2011), which has led to a rise in real wages and a greater demand for foreign labour (Park et al., 2010).

- Migrants come from developing countries and regions, such as North Korea, Viet Nam, South Asia and Africa (Skeldon, 2011).

- Migrants also come from the developed world: South Korea; Japan; Taiwan; Hong Kong, China; Europe; North America; and Australasia (*Ibid.*). Migrants from Australia have substantially increased since the 1900s, due to the return of the Chinese diaspora and the movement of skilled workers (Hugo, 2005). Likewise, North Americans, including the diaspora, are attracted by China's vibrant economy and low-cost living (Seligson, 2009; Sullivan, 2011; Pieke, 2012).

- Student migration to China is also on the rise – mostly from South Korea, the United States and Japan. China attracted 238,184 students from overseas in 2009 (more than those going to Canada and Australia) (Skeldon, 2011). China continues to send its own students abroad but growing numbers are returning upon completion of their studies. According to official Chinese statistics, over 186,000 returned in 2011; in the same year, for the first time, the number of returning students was more than half the number of outgoing students (OECD, 2012a).

31 The percentage of global migration represented by North–South flows varies depending on how countries are classified as North and South. When using either the World Bank or UNDP classification, this flow represents 3 per cent; under the UN DESA classification, it rises to 6 per cent.

32 UN DESA estimates that North–South migration remained roughly constant from 1990 to 2010, at around 13 million (United Nations General Assembly, 2012).

> • Despite signs of growing immigration, OECD (2012a) notes that China's enormous economic growth is not proportionately reflected in the number of foreigners working in the country. Unlike other countries, China lacks an official policy to attract skilled foreign workers.

Reliability of data

Capturing migration flows from North to South presents particular challenges, in addition to those encountered in measuring other flows of migration.

- Immigration statistics tend to be most comprehensive in OECD countries and other developed economies that have more established and reliable statistical records. In contrast, records of migrant stocks in developing countries are often outdated, incomplete or lacking entirely. Furthermore, when data do exist, comparability between countries is not always possible.

- Because of the paucity of data in migrant-receiving countries in the developing world, North–South migration is often studied by way of emigration flows from sending countries. In terms of international comparability, flows are generally problematic. Furthermore, leaving a country usually requires fewer administrative procedures than entering one, and outflow data are therefore less likely to be captured by the sending country. Consequently, measuring outflows is more problematic than measuring inflows (Lemaitre, 2005).[33]

- While it is likely that a considerable portion of North–South migration is composed of returning migrants or members of the diaspora, these flows may not be recorded at all or it may not be possible to separate them from total flows. Some countries, such as Brazil, are able to capture data on the stocks of returned migrants in censuses, by asking for the place of previous residence rather than the country of birth, although this presents its own set of complications.[34]

Migration drivers

Economic opportunity

The recent financial and economic crisis in the North and a growing demand for skilled labour in emerging economies in the South seem to be partly responsible for the increase in North–South migration. While traditional emigration countries in the South will continue to provide a large proportion of the world's workers, in the coming years, evidence suggests that workers from the North are also being drawn to new Southern destinations, such as BRICS countries[35] and emerging African and Latin American economies. Work permits granted to foreigners in Brazil increased by 64 per cent between 2009 and 2011, for example, with the largest single recipient group being US nationals in 2011 (MTE, 2012).

---

33 See www.oecd.org/migration/internationalmigrationpoliciesanddata/36064929.pdf for a discussion on the statistical challenges of migration measurement, particularly regarding flows.
34 See Barbosa de Campos, M. in Pinto de Oliveira, L.A. and A.T. Ribeiro de Oliveira, 2011:74.
35 Refers to Brazil, the Russian Federation, India, China and South Africa.

Expansion of global companies

Along with the independent migration of workers, companies are increasingly establishing themselves in the South, creating a growing number of international postings for skilled workers from the North. According to the *2012 Global Mobility Survey Report*, 47 per cent of organizations reported growth in international assignments in the previous year, fuelled partly by explosive expansion into emerging markets (Brazier, 2012). China is fast becoming the leading destination for international placements, with other BRIC economies also increasing in popularity. Other relocation surveys have yielded similar results, with up to 50 per cent more businesses indicating an increased number of placements between 2010 and 2011.[36] Global expansion may also contribute to return migration, as companies desire immigrants in the North who can return to work in their country of origin in the South with more cultural know-how and linguistic abilities (Cullen, 2007).

 Box 4

Migration to Brazil

- Migrants to Brazil increased by 87 per cent between the 1995/2000 and 2005/2010 census periods, with 268,295 arriving in the five years prior to the 2010 census (IBGE, 2012a).

- Between 2000 and 2010, the United States, Japan, Paraguay and Bolivia remained key source countries for migrants. The United States is now the top source country, with migration from there having increased by 212 per cent since the 2000 census (*Ibid.*). Portugal has increased in importance in the last 10 years, while Argentina has declined in importance.

- In 2011, the Ministry of Labour and Employment (MTE) granted 70,524 work permits to foreigners – up 64 per cent from the previous two years. Numbers from 2012 suggest that the trend will continue (MTE, 2012).

- Although many of the main nationalities receiving permits remain from 2004 – namely the United States, the Philippines, the United Kingdom, Germany, France, Italy and Japan – an increasing share is coming from the Philippines, India and Indonesia.

- There has been a strong increase in the number of Brazilians returning to their country of origin, with roughly twice as many recorded in 2010 as in the 2000 census (IBGE, 2012a). Japan, the United States and Portugal are particularly relevant source countries for return migrants, with Brazil-born individuals representing 89, 84 and 77 per cent of arrivals from these countries, respectively (*Ibid.*).

- As a share of the total immigrant population, the number of return migrants has increased slightly – from 61.2 per cent in the 2000 census to over 65 per cent in the 2010 census (*Ibid.*).

36 For instance, the 2012 Relocation Trends Survey, conducted by Brookfield Global Relocation Services, found that overseas assignments increased in 64 per cent of companies surveyed in 2011. See also Associates for International Research Inc. (AIRINC)'s 2011 *Mobility Outlook Questionnaire* (AIRINC, 2011).

Return migration

While return migration from the North in response to the financial crisis has likely been exaggerated in mainstream media, increased levels of return can be seen in several countries experiencing strong growth. In Brazil, 175,766 individuals (65 per cent of international immigrants) were return migrants in 2010 – roughly twice the number recorded in the 2000 census.[37] Countries sending back large numbers of migrants include Japan, the United States and Portugal (IBGE, 2012a). Return migration to China of both first- and second-generation migrants is also significant, with large numbers coming from North America and Australasia (Hugo, 2005). Historic shifts in migration between Mexico and the United States are also taking place, with net migration reaching zero in the United States in 2010, partly due to an increase in return flows (Passel Cohn and Gonzalez-Barrera, 2012).

 Box 5

South Korean migration to the Philippines (North–South)

- The number of South Koreans arriving in the Philippines has exploded by nearly 430 per cent in the past decade – from around 175,000 in 2000 (8.78% of all arrivals), to 925,000 in 2011 (nearly 25% of all arrivals and the largest group, ahead of the United States, Japan and China) (Department of Tourism, Philippines).

- Increasing numbers of foreign visitors are opting to extend their stay. In the first half of 2011, the Bureau of Immigration (2011a) approved a total of 81,287 applications for extension – an increase of 34 per cent, compared with the same period in 2010.

- Aside from tourists, long-stayer migrants include students, business people, traders and missionaries.

- There are 115,000 Koreans residing permanently in the Philippines (Legarda, 2011). Most intend to stay only temporarily but tend to come and go (Miralao and Makil, 2007).

- Korean students are one of the largest groups, with many going there to study English. More than 61,601 foreigners were studying in the Philippines in 2011 (Bureau of Immigration, 2012), with Koreans topping the list of foreigners in elementary and high schools and short-term courses in 2010 (Bureau of Immigration, 2011b). Koreans are also the largest group holding 9(F) student visas, which are used for enrolment in tertiary education programmes.

Student migration

A growing number of students are choosing to pursue education abroad and, increasingly, they are opting to do so outside of traditional destination countries. According to the UNESCO Institute for Statistics (UIS) (2012), there were roughly

---

37 Return migration, while increasing in number, has constituted a roughly constant share of total inflows over the past decade. These data measure Brazilians who were residing outside Brazil on a fixed date, five years prior to the 2010 census, and thus capture only returns that occurred in the five years prior to the census. Figures for 2000 were derived using the same fixed date method.

3.4 million internationally mobile students[38] in 2009 – a threefold increase from the 1.1 million recorded in 1980. Although over three quarters of foreign students were in OECD countries in 2008, the number studying in non-OECD destinations is growing faster than the growth rate of students entering the OECD, reflecting the increased diversity of destination choices beyond traditional receiving countries (OECD, 2010b).[39] New countries in the South that have emerged as popular destinations for international students include China, Malaysia and South Africa (UIS, 2012).

 Box 6

---

38 The UIS defines internationally mobile students as those who study in a foreign country of which they are not a permanent resident (UNESCO, 2009). Student flows presented here include only data where both receiving and sending country information is available, thus totals are substantially lower than in reality.

39 OECD data refer to students who do not hold the citizenship of the country for which the data are collected. Thus, they may include some permanent residents and cannot be directly compared to UIS data, which is more restrictive in its definition (see footnote 38) (OECD, 2010).

> Portugal has also witnessed growing emigration in recent years.
>
> - Emigration figures rose 41 per cent between 2009 and 2010 to 23,760. Of those captured by the Portuguese census in 2010, 93 per cent were of Portuguese nationality (INE Portugal, 2012).
>
> - In 2010, nearly 60,000 individuals born in Portugal resided in Africa, representing an increase of 42 per cent from a decade before, with the largest numbers in South Africa, Angola and Mozambique (UN DESA, 2012b).

Retirement migration

A recognized form of migration from the North to the South is the flow of retirees moving in search of warmer climates and cheaper living in the developing world. Popular flows to the South include American and Canadian migration to Mexico and other destinations in Latin America and the Caribbean; for Europeans, new destinations include Bulgaria, Romania and Turkey, although flows remain much smaller than those to traditional destinations in the Mediterranean and other areas of Southern Europe; other flows in Europe often follow along colonial ties – for instance, British retirees moving to South Africa; in South-East Asia, Thailand, Malaysia and the Philippines have emerged in the last two decades as retirement locations – for example, for the aging Japanese population.[40] In one example, the number of United States-born residents aged 55 and over increased substantially in both Mexico and Panama between 1990 and 2000, rising by 17 per cent in Mexico and 136 per cent in Panama during this period (Dixon et al., 2006).

Potential development impacts

Although still a small percentage of global migratory flows, North–South migration may have significant impacts on host societies and development that remain understudied. While little research exists, it is likely that migrants from the North can bring both human and financial capital to their new communities, and can contribute to a 'reverse brain drain' through the sharing of skills and knowledge. Furthermore, migrants from the North who move to the South create new linkages and networks across borders that may be rich in technical knowledge, as well as financial and political resources. Wealthy migrants from the North may also stimulate the service industry, may buy or rent homes, consume goods, and attract greater investments and more foreign visitors to developing regions (Dixon et al., 2006). Many developing countries are also increasingly trying to engage with their diasporas and to encourage skilled migrants to return home (IOM/MPI, 2012).

While migration from the North may have potential benefits, it is likely that not all impacts on host societies are positive. The presence of migrants from the North may drive up real estate prices, place increasing demands on already scarce

40 For the United States, Mexico and Panama, see Dixon et al., 2006; O'Reilly and Benson, 2009; for Japan, see Toyota, 2007 and Ono, 2008; for Turkey, see Balkır and Kırkulak, 2009.

health and social care services, and take jobs away from the local labour force. Furthermore, little is known about the social and cultural impacts of Northern migrants, particularly in areas where foreigners are concentrated in small cities or neighbourhoods. Finally, many new destinations in the South (such as Brazil, China and the Philippines) are traditionally characterized by *emigration*, and may not be fully prepared to meet the challenges of – or to benefit fully from – increasing flows *into* their countries. In sum, very little research has looked at the impacts of North–South migration on individuals or on migrant-receiving or -sending societies. Further investigation is required for a better understanding of the likely varied and, at times, contradictory impacts of this migration trend.

CONCLUDING REMARKS

As this chapter has shown, much is known about migration pathways in terms of the numbers involved, the direction of movement and migrant characteristics. An in-depth review of migration data sheds light on some overlooked trends – for instance, migration from South to South, or North to South – and highlights the need to examine their implications for development. This chapter sets the scene for the next two chapters, which take a more migrant-focused world view, examining the migration experience from a more qualitative perspective.

 Migrant Voices

Building a career: Spanish migrant working in Buenos Aires, Argentina (North–South)

Pablo originally moved to Buenos Aires to pursue a Master's degree in Creative Advertising nearly two years ago, drawn by the city's strong reputation for excellence in his chosen field – in terms of both academic quality and the level of professionals working in marketing and publicity. Additionally, an education in Argentina was much less expensive than a comparable degree in Spain.

After finishing his degree, Pablo decided to remain in Buenos Aires to pursue professional opportunities. At first, he found it very difficult to find a job without his residency permit and he was obliged to intern in several companies in order to boost his qualifications. Eventually, after quite a struggle, Pablo was hired by a multinational company that provided him with the necessary documents to gain temporary residence for one year, with the possibility of extension.

Pablo loves his job as a creative editor, saying he is 100 per cent satisfied. While there are few differences between working in Spain and Argentina, Pablo observes that, in Argentina, people work longer hours because of their strong drive to earn bonuses and move ahead in their careers. When asked if it is his ideal work, Pablo half-jokingly responds that the perfect job would be in the open air – for instance, as an instructor of surfing or some high-risk sport – but that what he has is second best. Pablo lives within his means, saying he cannot afford to waste too much, but he has enough for food, housing and leisure time. In Spain, Pablo remarks, it is impossible to have economic independence and, in this sense, his situation has improved since the move.

Pablo lives in the small Chinatown area in the north of Buenos Aires and feels comfortable and safe in his community. Many of his neighbours are also young immigrants from Spain, which helps to create a supportive network. While Pablo feels welcome in Argentina, he is aware that it is not the same for all nationalities. While Pablo's girlfriend is from Argentina, his closest friends are mainly Chilean and Spanish, and he feels an especially close bond with other Spanish people. He likes the sociable, out-going nature of Argentineans most of all but says this can be too much, sometimes, as well!

Pablo is satisfied with the health care available to him in Buenos Aires and reports being healthy. He appreciates the professional opportunities available to him and the high quality of his working environment. He enjoys getting to know people from all over Latin America and the world, and appreciates the proximity of places such as Brazil and Peru, which would be very hard to visit from Spain. The most challenging thing about living abroad is being far from his family and friends in Spain: "You become a little more guarded, a little cold," he says. However, Pablo is happy with his life and with his decision to move, although he says the move is only temporary. In the future, he sees himself returning to Spain and living in Barcelona.

Chapter 3

Review of studies on migration, happiness and well-being

David Bartram with IOM
(Frank Laczko, Rudolf Anich and Christine Aghazarm)

HIGHLIGHTS

Concepts and measures of migrant well-being and happiness can provide useful indicators of human development, as it has increasingly been recognized that development cannot be measured simply in terms of economic indicators such as economic growth and gross domestic product (GDP). Since migrants often leave their homes in search of a better life, measures of subjective well-being can provide an indication of whether migrants achieve their goal.

While recent years have seen a growing interest among social scientists and policymakers in happiness as an indicator of social progress, research on the links between migration and happiness or subjective well-being is in its infancy.

Research on happiness has looked at a range of factors – particularly the links between income and happiness. Findings suggest that although people with higher incomes are generally happier, once a certain threshold is reached, it seems to make little difference in terms of continuing increases in happiness. Other research shows that people living in high-income countries are happier than those living in low-income countries. This indicates that a certain level of economic development is necessary and can make a difference to the levels of happiness and well-being in a population. Other factors, such as good health, vibrant social networks, religious belief and old age, for example, are also shown to have a positive effect on levels of happiness.

This research on happiness has been minimal in lower-income countries, particularly with regard to migrants. Available research suggests that, overall, migrants are less happy than comparable populations in the country of destination and happier than similar populations back home who did not migrate. It might be expected that happiness increases, over time, as migrants become more integrated into the host society, but several studies in Europe have found that migrants remain less happy than native populations, even many years after migration.

For some vulnerable groups of migrants, the circumstances and drivers of migration have an acute effect on their psychosocial well-being. Those who migrate in extreme circumstances – for example, fleeing conflict and humanitarian crises – such as refugees and stranded migrants or those caught in trafficking and smuggling movements, may experience much suffering and trauma along the way, which continues to reverberate in their lives, once in the country of destination.

This chapter reviews the results of studies on happiness and well-being. It considers the methodological challenges involved in such research, and considers how and whether these concepts are applicable to the field of international development. The chapter reviews the literature on well-being, in general, and looks particularly at the influence of income as a factor, followed by a brief review of other aspects. It then focuses on the available research on migrants, which compares their well-being with that of the population of the destination country as well as of the country of origin. It concludes with a look at the well-being of families left behind, as well as migrants in difficult circumstances.

BACKGROUND

As noted in chapter 1, policymakers and scholars are showing an increasing interest in measuring the happiness and well-being of populations. This chapter considers the methodological challenges in researching this topic, and the findings of studies undertaken so far on the factors influencing the happiness of people, especially migrants. It sets the scene for the original research data on migrant well-being, which are presented in chapter 4.

Academic research on happiness has expanded particularly in the last two decades. Early contributions came from economists interested in the connections between happiness and economic growth, as well as psychologists more recently wishing to counterpoise a long-standing tradition of emphasis by psychologists on mental illness and psychological dysfunction. Interest among sociologists and others is more recent (but see Veenhoven, 1984, 1991, and Inglehart, 1997). The study of happiness nonetheless remains in its infancy and is beset by methodological challenges.

Methodological challenges

The first challenge lies in defining happiness as a component of well-being. The academic studies reviewed in this section have defined well-being in different ways or may have looked at related terms, such as quality of life, living standards, or human development. In some circles, well-being is understood to mean 'happiness', in particular, but it is in fact a broader concept. For instance, in this report, an individual's well-being is understood to encompass outcomes relating to career, health and social life, among others. There is no agreed definition of the terms 'well-being' or 'happiness' among communities of academics and policymakers involved in advancing this work (Bergheim, 2006:5). The terms are related but not identical.

Researchers have used a variety of definitions to capture how people feel about their quality of life, for example:

> Human wellbeing refers to a state of being with others, where human needs are met, where one can act meaningfully to pursue one's goals and where one enjoys satisfactory quality of life (definition of the Economic and Social Research Council (ESRC) Research Group on Wellbeing in Developing Countries, in Wright, 2011:1460).

Given the divergent uses of these terms, the literature review carried-out here does not use narrow definitions; the net is cast widely to consider all such terms and to bring them under the umbrella of 'well-being'.

The second challenge involves data collection and analysis. Research on happiness relies primarily on quantitative analysis of survey data. Several key surveys (such as the World Values Survey and the European Social Survey) include questions aimed at evoking an overall evaluation of respondents' happiness. Such questions might include, for example: "Taking all things together, how happy would you say you are?", and would be answered on a scale of (usually) 0 to 10. Some studies use more elaborate multi-item scales, based on answers to several questions. However, in terms of survey measures, at least, the data obtained are not notably different from the data resulting from a single question. Survey data on life satisfaction/happiness derived from single-item, self-reporting survey questions is seen as offering 'moderate' levels of validity (Diener et al., 1999; Veenhoven, 1993) and therefore useful in identifying the determinants of happiness (but not so useful when trying to compare happiness levels across different countries). Such survey data have a number of limitations:

- As with all surveys, there is sensitivity to question construction and question order. Other methodologies – for instance, asking respondents to keep diaries recording their own impressions of happiness – may help overcome some of the limitations of conventional surveys (Kahneman et al., 2004).

- Their usefulness for international comparisons of happiness levels across different countries is inhibited by cultural variation. It is commonly agreed that the different definitions of the word 'happiness', coupled with the issue of different cultures having different meanings and different ways of answering survey questions, represent an under-explored area (Oishi, 2010).

- Most research on well-being is conducted on wealthy countries, partly because the quality of the data is usually higher (Graham, 2009). This leads to reasonable questions about the extent to which this research can provide insights into the experiences of people living in poorer countries, especially when looking at migration from poor to rich countries.

- There is a lack of longitudinal data on migrants and happiness or life satisfaction – that is, data collected at several points in time on the same individuals. For migrants, this would mean collecting data before and after migration takes place. Surveys that involve returning to the same individuals (namely, panel data, usually collected at a quarterly or annual interval) often form part of national endeavours, such as the British Household Panel Survey. These surveys are usually inadequate, in terms of capturing data on immigrants, and they do not collect any data on immigrants prior to their arrival at their destination. Nor is this information collected by countries of origin: those who emigrate tend to be lost to national censuses or household surveys, despite increasing attempts to collect information about household members living abroad. Most existing analysis is therefore limited to cross-sectional comparisons comparing different individuals at one point in time – for example, comparing immigrants to natives or migrants to stayers.

- Happiness measures are not yet finding their way into established development surveys, despite their potential usefulness (see Graham, 2011; Blanchflower and Oswald, 2005). Efforts to develop new indicators that include the subjective consequences of objective elements of development (Schimmel, 2009), such as the New Economics Foundation's Happy Planet Index (Thompson et al., 2007), have not gained as much currency as the Human Development Index. A detailed discussion of the challenges of measuring happiness internationally can be found in academic literature.[41]

41 See, for example, chapter 2 of: Helliwell, J., R Layard and J. Sachs (eds), 2012, *World Happiness Report*. Available from www.earth.columbia.edu/sitefiles/file/Sachs%20Writing/2012/World%20Happiness%20Report.pdf.

Implications for development

Defining social progress in terms of a population's well-being has implications for development and has been debated by academics and migration practitioners. Some argue that subjective measures of well-being are less important than objective indicators such as, for example, income, poverty, health and employment. Thus, for the world's poorest people, for whom survival cannot be taken for granted, happiness is seen as secondary to more fundamental development concerns such as food security and the prevention of disease. The argument loosely follows the reasoning of twentieth-century psychologist Abraham Maslow's 'hierarchy of needs' theory, whereby human beings must first meet their basic survival needs, in the form of water, food and warmth, followed by safety. Once these needs are met, human beings seek the fulfilment of psychological needs, such as belonging, love and esteem. Finally, there is 'self-actualization' – a desire to achieve one's full potential and purpose.

While it is clear that the purpose of development is to afford people the ability to fulfil basic needs, once these needs are met, there is less agreement on what constitutes a development concern. Moreover, there might be a risk to the development agenda in over-emphasizing subjective happiness and minimizing the importance of material wealth. Others refer to the so-called 'happy peasants' idea (people are happy with little so there is no need for development) as a reason for maintaining inequality between peoples. On the other hand, there has also been a long tradition in development circles of resisting the idea that development simply means economic growth, with a view to countries and citizens becoming ever richer. Instead, economic growth should be seen as a means of achieving more fundamental goals.

There is increasing debate about the fundamental goals that should underpin development policy. The capability approach, for example, emphasizes the goal of enhancing people's 'freedoms' on the basis that freedom itself is a fundamental goal, valuable in its own right (Sen, 1999). It is therefore important to address conditions such as malnutrition and disease that undermine people's capability, agency and ability to act for themselves. A similar point can be made about other development concerns, such as a lack of education and a lack of health care. Economic growth may help address these more fundamental concerns, but it is not an end in itself. If these concerns can be addressed by other means (for instance, through changes in habits or customs), then economic growth becomes, to some extent, even less central to the development agenda.

The 'capability approach' represents a significant advance in thinking beyond conventional notions of development that focus on economic growth. It has been applied, to some degree, in the Human Development Index (HDI), which incorporates measures of health and education, as well as per-capita GDP. However, there is an increasing awareness of the need to go further, in terms of identifying what counts as fundamental to development. Freedoms and capabilities, as embodied in health and education and the like, are certainly valuable in their own right, but they are also valuable insofar as they contribute to happiness. In this sense, the debate on well-being and happiness is relevant to the development agenda.

FACTORS INFLUENCING WELL-BEING

A wide range of factors affecting well-being have been studied. Recent initiatives by national and international agencies, such as the OECD *How's Life* report, have looked at financial situation, employment, housing conditions, exposure to air pollution, life expectancy, education and crime, over the past 15 years. Likewise, the UK Measuring National Well-being Programme (MNW), launched in 2010, sought to move beyond economic indicators to measures of life quality and well-being.

Income and happiness

Researchers have shown a particular interest in looking at how income affects happiness, especially with the growing focus of policymakers in this area. Some contend that, at least above a certain threshold, an ever-higher income contributes little to happiness (Easterlin, 1974, 2001; Scitovsky, 1992; Blanchflower and Oswald, 2004).

Findings from the OECD and British Government initiatives also suggest that personal wealth is not an overriding factor in determining well-being.

- The UK Measuring National Well-being Programme (MNW) found that, despite increasing financial hardship since the economic crisis of 2008, levels of self-reported life satisfaction have remained broadly stable throughout the last decade.

- The OECD *How's Life* study also confirms that well-being has increased over the past 15 years, although there is considerable variance among OECD countries and population groups. This resonates well with 'folk wisdom' – the 'money can't buy happiness' idea – despite the fact that the pursuit of wealth remains a goal for many residents of wealthy countries (Frank, 1999) and a central tenet of economic policy.

Easterlin's work has delved more deeply into this issue. The 'Easterlin paradox' found that, while a 'snapshot' comparison of individuals shows that people with higher incomes are happier than those with less income, increases in income over time do not appear to raise average levels of happiness (Easterlin, 1974). This is especially apparent from data on Japan: the very impressive growth of the Japanese economy, starting in the 1950s, did not result in greater happiness, even after several decades (Easterlin, 1995).

One explanation for the paradox is the idea of relative wealth and the links between income and status: it is not the absolute purchasing power of income that matters but the way it embodies and signals status (Clark et al., 2008). Those with higher incomes are happier than those with less, partly due to 'social comparisons' – the ability to compare favourably with others and to enjoy a perceived higher status. Researchers have further found that these comparisons tend to be relatively 'local' (Firebaugh and Schroeder, 2009); in other words, people compare their wealth and status with people around them, rather than with people from different countries.

Aspirational thinking is another factor. Studies have revealed that people continue to strive for increasingly higher income – a point that holds true not only among the poor, but also among those with relatively high incomes (Stutzer, 2003).

Indeed, aspirations are linked to the notion of comparative and relative wealth: those who gain a higher income (and status) begin to compare themselves to a higher reference group, instead of gaining satisfaction by comparing themselves to a stable reference group (Boyce et al., 2010) – the popular 'keeping up with the Joneses' mentality. While increases in income can lead to short-term spurts in happiness, the desire for ever-more income is insatiable, and research shows that people end up reverting to previous levels of well-being.

Another body of research disputes these findings and reasserts the role of economic wealth in achieving happiness. Ruut Veenhoven's 'liveability' theory (1995) offers an important contrasting framework: happiness is determined mainly by whether a person can meet his/her own needs. In this respect, wealthier countries are more liveable and provide better conditions for people to meet their needs and thus achieve happiness. Veenhoven's analysis casts doubt on whether social comparisons are an important factor in happiness.

In the development context, these ideas can be explored further by comparing national economic growth rates to the happiness of populations. The findings from the poll suggest a broad alignment between GDP and happiness – for example, Western Europe is higher up the scale than Africa – but the correlation is not absolute and there are anomalies, with developing countries such as Mexico or India being similar to, or higher than, Japan in their happiness ranking.

Some recent critiques of Easterlin's perspective indicate that happiness changes over time and in tandem with economic growth (or decline). For instance, Stevenson and Wolfers (2008) found that, when looking at the relationship between happiness and GDP per capita, out of 89 countries that saw changes in these measures, happiness and GDP per capita changed in the same direction in 62 cases (53 showing growth in both, 9 showing declines in both), whereas they moved in opposite directions in 27 cases (20 reflecting economic growth unaccompanied by growth in happiness, and 7 reflecting growing happiness, despite economic decline).

Easterlin and his colleagues (2010), however, identified a number of flaws in these studies and repeated their conclusion that, over the long term (more than 10 years), economic growth does not bring greater happiness. In his recent work, Easterlin (2010) presents new evidence that extends this finding to developing countries: for China, in particular, happiness has remained 'flat' (unchanged) despite very rapid economic growth. Similarly, Graham (2009) finds that determinants of happiness in poorer countries are much the same as determinants in wealthier countries. In Peru, for instance, the majority of people at every income level believed that they would need twice as much as their current income to live well and, in one survey, almost half of those who had experienced significant economic advance said that their situation was worse than it was 10 years ago (Graham, 2005).

Survey data from the United Republic of Tanzania also support the idea that the relative dimension of income matters greatly, even in quite poor countries (Kenny, 2005). Examples exist of poor countries that have seen increases in happiness, despite little or no economic growth. Kenny (Ibid.) suggests that some factors contributing to happiness (such as health and education) have, over time, been improving in poor countries for reasons other than economic growth. Some economists go further and find signs of an 'unhappy growth paradox', whereby countries with a higher growth rate (compared with countries at similar levels of development) show a lower average reported happiness (Lora and Chaparro, 2009).

In summary, although there is some contradictory evidence from different studies, the overriding message seems to be that, as far as the world's poorer countries are concerned, economic development is a necessity, in terms of meeting the basic needs and rights of citizens and enabling them to lead fulfilled lives, with greater happiness and well-being.

Other factors affecting well-being

Other well-researched dimensions of happiness include health, social networks, familial relations, and employment.

- Ball and Chernova (2008) show that employment and having a spouse/partner are particularly important happiness factors.

- Participating in social activities with friends, and/or having friends to confide in, is also a relevant factor (Bechetti et al., 2008; Sullivan, 1996).

- Another key determinant is health, which can include 'subjective health' – the perception that one's health is good.

- Religious people are generally happier than non-religious people, although that finding might pertain only to people who live in more religious contexts (Eichhorn, 2011).

- Age is also a significant factor, with decreased happiness occurring towards middle age, followed by an increase towards old age, although this might be offset by the fact that health declines with age.[42]

- Happiness is also affected by contextual factors such as employment protection and unemployment insurance (Boarini et al., 2012; Frey and Stutzer, 2002).

As with studies on income, researchers have found subtleties and paradoxes. For example, people with intimate partners are notably happier than those who are single, but while many people experience significant increases in happiness upon acquiring a partner (or getting married), some then find that, in due course, their happiness returns to previous levels (Lucas et al., 2003).

Direction of causality

An important question that emerges in happiness studies relates to the direction of causation: are people happy because of external acquisitions or are people who are intrinsically happier more successful in the external world (for example, better at finding partners or satisfying careers)? Research shows that those who are more satisfied in their jobs are happier, but evidence also suggests that happiness is just as likely to result in career satisfaction (Boehm and Lyubomirsky, 2008). Unemployment, on the other hand, has obvious implications for happiness; it has a negative effect on happiness levels that usually persists even after a person has found another job (Clark and Oswald, 1994; Lucas et al., 2004).

42 For broader reviews of determinants of happiness, see Dolan et al., 2008, and Diener et al., 2009a.

Some research has focused on how people are able to enhance their own happiness by changing their circumstances. This may relate to an evaluation of intrinsic versus extrinsic goals (Sheldon and Lyubomirsky, 2006) – for example, people may work to earn an income, motivated by the need for money rather than by the intrinsic satisfaction derived from the work itself. But if an increased income is gained by taking a job that involves longer hours or a longer commute, the happiness benefit of the extra income might well be small in comparison to the costs. A more favourable outcome might flow from taking a lower-paid job that involves more enjoyable work. Likewise, happiness might be enhanced by spending more time with one's spouse or partner doing activities that bring shared enjoyment (Sullivan, 1996).

In any event, researchers also recognize that happiness is not always related to externally controllable choices and circumstances. A significant proportion of variation in individual happiness levels is attributable to genetic predisposition, or personality (see Lykken and Tellegen, 1996; Schnittker, 2008), which may affect the ability of an individual to cope with, and adapt to, external circumstances. Since it is not always possible to change one's circumstances, however, individual happiness may result from a conscious change of approach or state of mind – as demonstrated by various philosophical and religious traditions (see, for example, Csikszentmihalyi, 1997 on Buddhism).

 Migrant Voices

Stranded in Somalia: Ethiopian migrant seeking a new life in the Middle East (South–North)

Life is hard in Bossaso. Despite a clear turquoise sea, white sands and friendly locals, brutal 45° heat, ongoing tension and cracked, arid land threaten the livelihoods of thousands. Buildings are left unfinished and become derelict, debris clutters neglected roads, and basic services are lacking. "The water is so dirty here. It is like seawater. Sometimes I even go a day or two without food," says Mustariya, who is currently suffering from severe stomach pains.

Originally from Ethiopia, Mustariya Mohamad is a 19-year-old woman who has been in Bossaso, the Puntland State of Somalia, for over a year. Leaving north-east Ethiopia to find prosperity in the Middle East, Mustariya embarked on a 15-day journey: "Nine of us left Ethiopia for Somalia – all from the same village. At first, it was easy; we paid some small money and a truck driver took us across the border. Then everything changed. Armed men stopped us, took us away and did bad things. They left the men alone; they just wanted us, the women. They held us hostage and stole everything we had, then spat us out on the side of the road. Our truck driver had left, so we had to walk for a week until we reached Bossaso."

After her traumatic journey, Mustariya arrived in Bossaso with no access to health care, psychosocial support or money: "I still want to see a doctor, but I can't go to the hospital because it is too expensive. Even finding a job here is difficult because I do not speak Somali, only Oromo. Once I had a cleaning job, but I could not understand my manager's instructions so he dismissed me." Mustariya is intent on reaching Yemen. The lure of prosperity, education and work in the Middle East is driving thousands of Ethiopians to pass through Somalia in search of good fortune. Crossing the Gulf of Aden, however, is a perilous journey: "The sea is very expensive to cross; it will cost me USD100 or USD150 to travel from Bossaso to Yemen. I know the problems; I know people die crossing the sea and many are deported, but I have been told Yemen will offer me a better life. I will do whatever it takes."

Mustariya is now being helped by a Migration Response Centre established jointly by the International Organization for Migration (IOM) and the Government of the Puntland, Somalia to register new migrants, provide a space for advocacy and migrant rights awareness, offer legal advice and provide medical referrals. But Hussein Hassan, IOM's Programme Officer in Somalia, says: "The need is vast; psychosocial support, clean water, shelter and a comprehensive migrant-friendly health-care package must be offered for the most vulnerable." As Mustariya leaves the Migration Health Response Centre for her evening prayers, she says: "I just want to find somewhere with peace – somewhere I can get an education. Am I asking for too much?"

Note: Adapted from Ethiopia/Somalia: "Migrating will offer me a better life. I will do whatever it takes". In: *IOM Gender and Migraton News*, pp.38, 2012.

RESEARCH ON MIGRATION AND HAPPINESS

The limited research on migrant well-being focuses on assessing migrant happiness, compared to the native population of the destination country and of the country of origin. Some studies have also explored the well-being of families left behind or of internal migrants.

Migrant well-being compared to that of the destination country population

Studies conducted mainly in developed countries typically show that migrants are, on average, less happy than native populations (Safi, 2010). This holds true even when other variables are controlled, such as when comparing migrants to natives who have the same characteristics or circumstances – the same income, employment status, relationship status, health and so on. It might be expected that happiness would increase over time as migrants assimilate into new societies, but this is not so, according to Safi's research on immigrants in Europe, which found that immigrants generally remained less happy than the native population, even many years after migration. However, some research conducted in developing and developed countries suggests that the happiness scores for migrants and non-migrants are very similar (see, for instance, UNDP, 2009; Graham, 2005; Kenny, 2005).

There may be various reasons for this. A key contributor could be that migrants tend to be less satisfied with their financial situation, even when earning incomes comparable to those of native populations (Bartram, 2011). Migrants to the United States, for example (even those who originate in poorer countries), have average earnings on a par with those of natives. They have succeeded in increasing their incomes, relative to pre-migration levels, but are nonetheless more dissatisfied with their incomes than are the natives. In addition, migrants also show a stronger association between income and happiness than do native residents, and are often more willing to take risks and be more entrepreneurial.

Migrants may also find themselves in a situation of lowered social status. Some migrants, despite being economically successful, may nevertheless find their relative position in the destination country lower than it was in their country of origin. Those with good educational qualifications and careers prior to migration may find that these achievements are not recognized in the destination country. They may encounter discrimination and/or language difficulties. The net outcome after migration could be higher income in 'absolute' terms (that is, in comparison to pre-migration income, after currency conversion) but a lowered social status in the destination country – with predictable consequences for the happiness quotient (Aycan and Berry, 1996). The challenges of the migrant experience itself will also affect levels of happiness (Handlin, 1973). Other possible explanations for lower levels of happiness might include separation from family and the challenge of adjusting to a new culture, but there are no data available to confirm this.

Migrant well-being compared to that of the country of origin population

Comparing the levels of happiness among migrants and native populations in destination countries is perhaps not the best way of assessing whether migrants' happiness has changed as a consequence of moving to another country. Apart from anything else, there may be engrained differences in the happiness levels of populations in different countries, which could skew the findings.

It is probably more useful to compare migrants with similar people who remain in their country of origin and choose not to migrate. Looking at data collected by the European Social Survey (ESS), it appears that those who have migrated from Eastern Europe to Western Europe are significantly happier than 'stayers', although there is little information as to why this might be the case (Bartram, 2012a). One reason might be that those who choose to migrate are happier to start with. Other studies (such as Graham and Markowitz, 2011) suggest that the converse may be true: an analysis of survey data from Latin America showed that people who expressed an intention to migrate (and eventually did migrate) were less happy than those lacking such an intention; although the migrants' situations were objectively seen to be favourable, the migrants were nonetheless dissatisfied, becoming what Graham and Markowitz call "frustrated achievers".

The difference in happiness between migrants and stayers may also depend on which country they originate from. For instance, the research on migration from Eastern to Western Europe reveals that migrants originating in certain countries (Croatia, the Russian Federation, Turkey and Ukraine) are happier than the stayers in those countries, whereas migrants from other countries (such as Romania) appear to be no happier than the stayers (Bartram, 2012b).

Well-being of migrant families back home

Some studies (such as Gartaula et al., 2012; Dreby, 2010) have looked at the well-being of migrants' family members left behind in the origin country and whether the benefits gained from remittances are sufficient to outweigh the subjective costs arising from family separation. Such studies have come up with variable findings. Research from Nepal shows that the context of women left behind by migrant husbands makes a difference to the wives' subjective sense of well-being. The women may experience greater well-being if they become the de facto head of the household, in their husbands' absence, and enjoy a greater sense of empowerment and control over their lives. Equally, well-being may improve through an increase in household income as a result of remittances, especially in the case of very poor families (Gartaula et al., 2011). On the other hand, subjective well-being may not improve and may even decline if, for example, women have to live with their in-laws during their husbands' absence, and/or when the pre-migration financial situation was comfortable enough that remittances resulted in only a small financial improvement.

Research in the United States (Dreby, 2010), though not framed explicitly in terms of happiness, also shows quite clearly the emotional costs of family separation, particularly for children left in the care of other family members. Findings from Ecuador further reinforce the conclusion that the benefits of remittances are often outweighed by the costs of separation (Borraz et al., 2007). By contrast, a survey in Latin America found that households with a remitting migrant abroad were happier than those without; it suggests that this difference might be explained by the way migration diversifies risk for the household (and thus perhaps enhances financial security, rather than simply raising income) (Cardenas et al., 2009). However, these studies do not consider the happiness of the absent migrant and, consequently, do not look at the happiness of the household as a whole.

Researchers have also looked at internal migration flows. Migration from Eastern to Western Germany may be instructive, as such movements can be likened to international migration, given that the two regions were separate countries from 1949 until 1990, despite the linguistic and cultural similarities. Melzer's (2011) study found that migrants moving from Eastern to Western Germany between 1990 and 2007 were happier after migration and happier than those who did not migrate. Research in China, by contrast, shows that rural-to-urban migrants are less happy than rural stayers and urban native residents (Knight and Gunatilaka, 2010). The study concludes that migrants probably felt disappointed because they did not anticipate that their aspirations would rise after migration (in line with the Easterlin perspective).

Circumstances of migration

The circumstances in which migration takes place inevitably affect migrants' levels of happiness. As noted, among those who migrate for economic reasons, increased income over a certain threshold does not necessarily lead to proportionately greater happiness. Whether this holds true for all migrants may depend on whether their earnings have already reached or exceeded that threshold (as per Easterlin).[43]

In the case of South–North and South–South movements, it is less clear whether migrants reach the requisite income threshold; coming from poor countries, they are less likely to have done so but it is also known that, relatively speaking, migrants tend to come from the better-off sections of society and are not the very poorest. There are no available data to indicate whether migrants themselves rate their well-being as greater or lesser, post-migration, although migrants' well-being has been compared with that of other population groups – native populations and stayers – as discussed above.

In other migration contexts, such as where asylum or refugee status is being sought,[44] the outcome may go either way. On the one hand, if migrants are not mainly focused on economic gain, they may experience less disappointment if economic outcomes in destination countries do not live up to expectations. On the other hand, they may carry heavy burdens from their country of origin – for example, if they are refugees escaping persecution and are forced to leave their homes – which may diminish their sense of well-being.

Much of the literature on the psychological well-being of refugees focuses on the negative mental health consequences of forced displacement, with a considerable body of work seeking to determine the prevalence of Post-Traumatic Stress Disorder and other mental illnesses (Murray et al., 2008). Research has also revealed that refugees are at risk of developing severe and long-lasting psychological and behavioural problems (Porter and Haslam, 2005). Variation in the mental health outcomes of refugees can be linked to the impact of numerous factors relating to both pre- and post-displacement circumstances, as well as the characteristics of the refugees themselves (*Ibid.*).

Positive psychology – an umbrella term for the study of positive emotions, positive character traits, and enabling institutions – has only recently been applied to refugees and, so far, little work directly addresses the effect of forced migration on happiness. Little research has been carried-out on happiness among refugees – only one study of Palestinian children in a West Bank camp (Veronese et al., 2012), which found that the children's happiness was similar to that of Palestinian children living in an Israeli village. In terms of returnees, a study comparing the happiness of Romanian return migrants to that of stayers (Bartram, 2012b) found that returnees are not happier than stayers, despite earning higher incomes.

---

43 See Kenny (2005) for a discussion on what that threshold might be.
44 International survey data sets, such as the European Social Survey (ESS), do not allow for learning about the motivations for migration. Some of the people analysed above might fit better in a category of 'family reunification' than in 'economic migration', and reasons for migrating are often multiple. The analysis of ESS data in the previous sections was constructed in ways designed to discern outcomes for people whose migration was likely motivated by a desire to improve their economic situation – a focus also evident in other research.

Chapter 3
Review of studies on migration,
happiness and well-being 100

While research may not directly measure happiness, a substantial amount of literature has been produced on the mental health of refugees, often focusing on the instance of negative psychological states/conditions.

Consistent and strong links have been made between pre-migration trauma and mental health in resettlement (Murray, 2008:6). Research tends to show the healing power of time, with the mental health of refugees in resettlement improving with time, especially as the initial stressors of resettlement subside.

A growing body of research shows that post-migration stressors can significantly affect the settlement of refugees (Murray et al., 2008) – stressors such as a decrease in socioeconomic status, the loss of meaningful social roles or life purpose, unemployment or economic hardship and social isolation, which negatively affect mental health and the ability to adapt (Murray et al., 2008:8). Post-migration difficulties may also be the result of a particular refugee's compatibility with the host culture, the nature of the resettlement programme (Murray et al., 2008), the attitude of the host community, and the educational services/systems for refugee children and adults. Overall, it is clear that the numerous pre- and post-migration factors result in a wide variety of mental health and integration outcomes among refugees (*Ibid.*).

CONCLUDING REMARKS

Research on migrants' well-being is relatively new but has gained more attention in recent times. The existing research has got to the heart of the matter, in terms of looking at the links between economic success and well-being, at the level of both individuals and nations. The findings suggest a clear link between economic growth and happiness, up to a point; once a certain threshold is reached, however, ever-increasing income appears to have less effect. This research provides a useful backdrop against which to test the findings of the Gallup poll in the next chapter.

 **Migrant Voices**

German graduate student in New York (North–North)

Interested in continuing her education, Vera recently began a Master's degree in film studies at a well-known university in New York. Attracted by the university's strong reputation and the vibrancy of its host city, Vera was also eager to experience living in another culture, particularly in the English-speaking world, hoping it would improve her attractiveness to employers further down the road. Studying in the United States also gave Vera more flexibility in her choice of programmes than she would have had in Germany. Several months into the programme, Vera is happy with her decision to move to the United States. While she admits that, at times, it is tough to be so far from home, she enjoys the academic rigour and intellectual environment and feels she is in the "right place".

The process of getting to the United States, and of gaining admission to such a highly competitive school, required considerable time, effort and money. "It felt like a long, long journey," Vera says. However, she was amazed by the level of support and personalized attention she received from the university and from her professors, even before she arrived.

Vera lives in what is jokingly known as "academic island" – an area of the city densely populated by students. She shares an apartment with students from the United States and says she always feels safe in her neighbourhood. The proximity to her classes and the peacefulness of the neighbourhood, which is dotted with parks, make the area pleasant to live in. Perhaps the nightlife is a little tame, but there is always a subway ride into the city for that. Vera has made several close friends and appreciates how diverse her social group is, with classmates coming from all over the United States and the world. Vera communicates with her family and friends in Germany via Skype, Facebook and letters.

While she enjoys her living situation and the high quality of her education, Vera knows that the opportunity does not come cheap. Even with two scholarships covering her EUR 18,000 annual tuition and more, Vera was obliged to take out a loan and to borrow from her mother to cover her expenses. She also works as a research and teaching assistant at her university, and as a writer for culture magazines in Germany. "I found it a little shocking that, even with scholarships, one could not afford this opportunity," she remarks. Luckily, thus far, Vera has been healthy and has not had to seek medical care; her friends' stories of large bills make her cautious about seeking medical care in the future.

While Vera is thankful for the opportunity and inspired by the high standard of the education she receives, she cannot be sure that the financial risk she has taken will pay off in the end. There is no guarantee of a job when she graduates, particularly as her field of study does not directly lead into a traditional career path. "It's a high risk to take," she admits, but one she is willing to go for. Despite excellent grades, Vera is unsure about her future. Following the completion of her degree, in another year and a half, she is considering pursuing a PhD – in the United States, the United Kingdom, or back in Germany. Asked if she ever plans to settle down in one place, Vera responds that the idea of settling seems "a bit out of date", somehow. "I don't live like that," she says, mentioning that she has also studied in Italy and Berlin. Although settling might not be the answer, for her, Vera understands the appeal. "The idea that I will never have a place that will be home is also very strange to me," she says.

Chapter 3
Review of studies on migration,
happiness and well-being 102

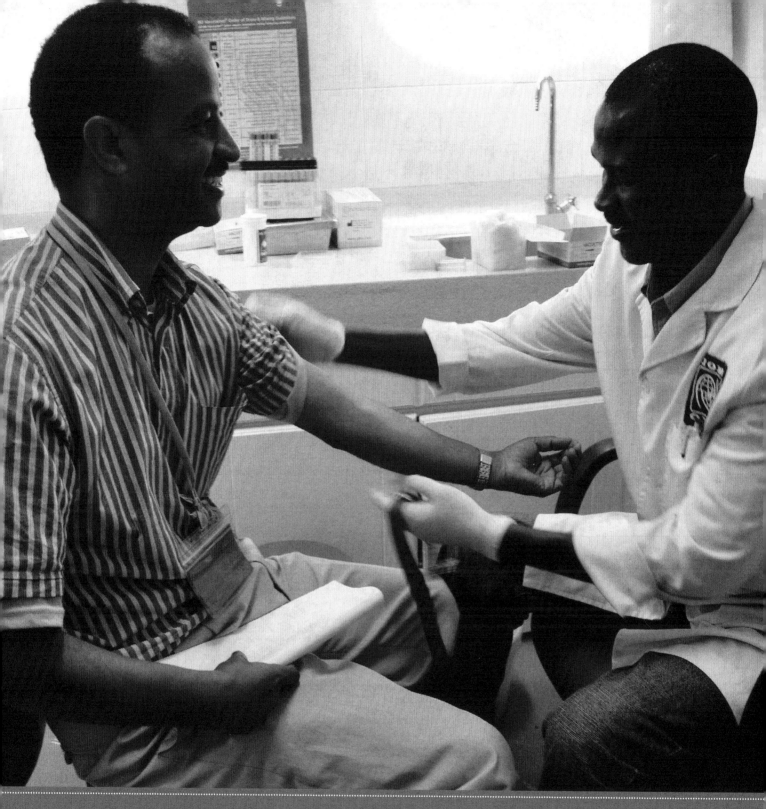

Chapter 4

Dimensions of migrant well-being: Evidence from The Gallup World Poll

Gallup
(Neli Esipova, Anita Pugliese, Julie Ray and Kirti Kanitkar)

4

HIGHLIGHTS[45]

Since 2005, Gallup's annual World Poll has been conducted in more than 150 countries, territories and regions, gathering opinions that are comparable across geographical areas and time. The data used in this analysis of migrant well-being were collected between 2009 and 2011, involving a survey of some half a million adults and including nearly 25,000 first-generation migrants and 441,000 native-born residents.

The poll assessed well-being by asking migrants about objective elements of their lives (such as income level, shelter, nutrition and employment opportunities), as well as about their own perceptions and feelings (such as life satisfaction, and positive and negative emotions). The survey also explored what migrants had gained and lost by migrating abroad, using a statistical model that compares migrant well-being in the destination country with what their lives might have been like had they stayed at home.

The findings reconfirm the divide between the rich and poor – the North–South divide. Whether migration improves well-being depends on where migrants come from and where they go to. Migrants moving from North to North appear to have the easiest experience. These migrants have the most positive outcomes in multiple dimensions of well-being, such as life satisfaction, emotional positivity, financial security, personal safety, community attachment and health.

By contrast, South–South migrants appear to face more significant challenges. They are the least optimistic about their lives and find it difficult to achieve a satisfactory standard of living. Furthermore, migration seems to make little difference to them financially. Personal safety is a concern. Moreover, migrants tend to lack confidence in the institutions of the country they have moved to, and tend to be troubled by their health.

Those migrating between the North and South, in either direction, have mixed experiences. Generally, economic factors play a particularly notable role: those migrating from the North to the South enjoy greater economic prowess, as might be expected for those moving to an environment with relatively low living costs. Conversely, those moving from the South to the North suffer from an economic disparity with the native-born; they struggle to make the transition but are nevertheless better off financially for having migrated than those who stayed at home.

---

45 The report adopts the terminology used in development discourse to categorize countries according to their economic status. This matter is discussed in detail in chapter 1 but, broadly speaking, 'North' refers to high-income countries and 'South' to low- and middle-income countries, as classified by the World Bank.

This chapter presents the findings of the Gallup World Poll on the well-being of migrants. It introduces the methodology of the study and then provides an analysis supported by data relating to financial, career, social, community, physical and subjective well-being.

INTRODUCTION TO THE GALLUP WORLD POLL

For the first time, Gallup's World Poll – the only global study of its kind – makes it possible to assess the well-being of migrants worldwide. Until now, most studies on migration and well-being have focused on migrant populations in specific countries or regions. Gallup annually asks the same questions, in the same way, in more than 150 countries, territories and regions (representing 98% of the world's total adult population), making it possible to compare data on migrants across multiple nations, regions and time.

This analysis draws on data collected between 2009 and 2011, based on a survey of nearly half a million adults and including roughly 25,000 first-generation migrants and 441,000 native-born residents. Gallup distinguishes migrants from the native-born by asking all respondents the straightforward question of whether they were born in the country they live in or not. Gallup classifies those who say "no" as first-generation migrants. By pooling data over three years, it is possible to create a robust sample of migrants for analysis (see box 10 for methodological details).

Although Gallup's World Poll surveys are not primarily designed to study migrants, the comprehensiveness of this global data set makes it possible to identify first-generation migrants and to study their lives and experiences in their destination countries. Data are adjusted with regard to age, sex and education to allow for fairer comparisons between migrants' well-being and the well-being of other populations, such as the native-born in destination countries.

This study shows that the well-being of migrants varies according to where the migrants live and where they come from. Gallup assesses the well-being of migrants based on self-reported information about their lives (including their evaluative and experiential well-being, as well as the financial, career, social, community and physical dimensions of their well-being). The study also explores what migrants have gained and lost through migration, comparing the well-being of migrants who have lived in a destination country for at least five years with estimates of what their lives might have been like had they stayed at home.

As discussed in chapter 1, international migration is often portrayed as a South–North phenomenon when, in fact, only about 40 per cent of all migrants move from developing countries in the South to more developed countries in the North. South–South migrants, for instance, are an important economic force, given the magnitude of their numbers and the remittances sent back home, but their lives and experiences are largely understudied. This 'blind spot' reflects the lack of reliable data on migrants who move from one developing country to another, as well as the heavy emphasis on South–North flows in policy debates and research (Ratha and Shaw, 2007). The wealth of data available from Gallup's ongoing global polling makes it possible, for the first time, to focus on all migration pathways: South–South, South–North, North–North and North–South.

The scale of international migration reported in the Gallup World Poll

In the absence of a universally agreed definition of 'South' and 'North', for the purposes of this analysis, 'North' represents high-income economies, based on World Bank classifications, and the 'South' represents low- and middle-income economies (see chapter 1 for more details). Gallup's estimates compare relatively well with the estimated distribution of global migrant stocks derived using UN

DESA, World Bank and UNDP definitions (see table 2 in chapter 2):[46] 40 per cent of migrants included in Gallup's sample moved from South to North, 33 per cent from South to South, 22 per cent moved from North to North, and 5 per cent moved from North to South (see figure 10).

 Figure 10   Gallup estimates of first-generation adult migrant stock, on the four pathways of migration, 2009–2011

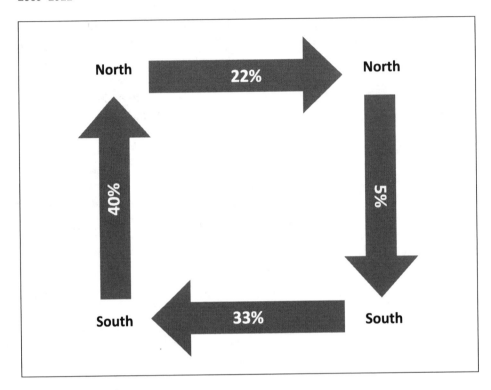

Source: Based on Gallup World Poll data, 2009–2011.
Note: Estimates include first-generation migrants aged 15 years or older.

The profile of migrants in the Gallup World Poll

Gallup data examine migrants on the basis of country of origin, duration of stay in the destination country, and key demographics (sex, age and education level) for each of the four pathways of migration. The methodology, determination of the sample, and definitions used are shown in boxes 9 and 10 at the end of this chapter.

The key characteristics of the population sample covered by this survey are as follows, with more data shown in tables 11 and 12:

Chapter 4
Dimensions of migrant well-being:
Evidence from the Gallup World Poll 108

46   The slight difference can be partly explained by the fact that Gallup's sample only includes migrants aged 15 years and older.

Country of birth

Gallup categorizes migrants as "from the North" or "from the South", based on their country of birth, using the World Bank classification. The migrants surveyed were born in the 188 countries (51 of which were in the North and 137 in the South) where the poll was conducted.

Duration of stay

Migrants are divided into two categories: newcomers (those who have moved to their destination country less than five years ago) and long-timers (those who have been living in their current country for at least five years). The two groups mirror how migrants are commonly classified in census data. Of all migrants in the sample, just over a quarter (27%) are newcomers and three quarters are long-timers.

Sex

- In the Gallup World Poll, there are no significant differences in the numbers of male and female migrants on any of the four migration pathways.

- Newcomers who move from South to North are only slightly more likely to be male, as are newcomers who move from North to South.

- Although past Gallup survey data are not available for comparison, this appears to confirm other research that suggests that the proportion of women migrating within the South is increasing – or, at least, that they are gaining on men, in terms of their numbers (Bakewell, 2009).

Age

- Newcomer migrants in the North tend to be younger than the native-born and long-timers, with nearly half (49% of those who have moved from North to North and 46% of those moving South to North) aged 15–29. Newcomer migrants in the South are also younger than the native-born.

- In the South, 30 per cent of long-timers who moved from North to South are aged 65 and older (compared with only 8% of the native-born in the South).

Education

- North–North migrants (particularly newcomers) are more educated than the native-born in the countries to which they move; they are nearly twice as likely (39%) to have a university degree as the native-born population (20%).

- South–North migrants, in comparison, are about as educated as, or slightly less educated than, the native-born in the North.

- On the other hand, South–North migrants are more likely to be highly educated than migrants who move from South to South.

- In the South, migrants are generally more educated than the native-born. For instance, 44 per cent or more of migrants in the South have completed 9–15 years of education, compared with 32 per cent of the native-born.

Table 11 Native-born and migrants in the North, by sex, age and education, 2009–2011

| | | Native-born in the North | Migrants in the North | | | |
| | | | North–North | | South–North | |
			Long-timers	Newcomers	Long-timers	Newcomers
SEX	Female	52%	55%	53%	53%	44%
	Male	48%	45%	47%	47%	56%
AGE	15–29	22%	17%	49%	27%	46%
	30–44	26%	23%	35%	35%	41%
	45–64	33%	35%	11%	27%	11%
	65+	19%	25%	5%	11%	2%
EDUCATION	4-year university degree	20%	26%	39%	21%	19%
	9–15 years of education	65%	60%	56%	61%	58%
	Primary school or less (up to 8 years of education)	15%	14%	5%	18%	23%

Copyright © 2012 Gallup, Inc. All rights reserved.
Source: Gallup World Poll data, 2009–2011.

 Table 12 Native-born and migrants in the South, by sex, age and education, 2009–2011

| | | Native-born in the South | Migrants in the South | | | |
| | | | South–South | | North–South | |
			Long-timers	Newcomers	Long-timers	Newcomers
SEX	Female	50%	54%	51%	51%	41%
	Male	50%	46%	49%	49%	59%
AGE	15–29	36%	23%	46%	31%	46%
	30–44	31%	25%	33%	18%	34%
	45–64	25%	30%	16%	21%	10%
	65+	8%	22%	5%	30%	10%
EDUCATION	4-year university degree	6%	13%	8%	15%	13%
	9–15 years of education	32%	45%	47%	44%	49%
	Primary school or less (up to 8 years of education)	62%	42%	45%	41%	38%

Copyright © 2012 Gallup, Inc. All rights reserved.
Source: Gallup World Poll data, 2009–2011.

Chapter 4
Dimensions of migrant well-being:
Evidence from the Gallup World Poll 110

GALLUP WORLD POLL METHODOLOGY

Analytical process

Gallup analyses migrants' well-being in several ways:

i) By comparing the self-reported well-being of migrants and the well-being of the native-born in the country of residence;

ii) By comparing the self-reported well-being of migrants in their country of residence and that of 'matched stayers' in their country of origin (with estimates of what their lives might have been like, had they stayed at home).

The first analysis examines how migrants' lives compare with those of the native-born in the destination country. To allow for a meaningful comparison between the native-born, long-timers and newcomers, data were adjusted by sex, age and education (see box 9 at end of the chapter for details).

The second analysis considers what migrants have gained and lost by migrating abroad. It sheds light on the extent to which migration can be beneficial or disadvantageous for migrants, in terms of personal human development. This analysis is possible because the Gallup World Poll surveys ask the same questions using consistent methodology worldwide. Using a statistical model that compares the lives of migrants with the lives of people with the same age, sex and education profile in their country of birth ('matched stayers'), it is possible to impute what migrants' lives hypothetically would have been like, had they stayed at home.

As any move causes a disruption in a person's life, only long-timers who have had five years to settle into their host country are considered for the second analysis. Gallup assigned each long-timer respondent a set of 'imputed' responses, based on the Gallup World Poll surveys in his or her country of birth, using respondents of the same sex, age and education level (for details, see box 9).

Gallup's definition of well-being

Gallup's well-being metrics (widely quoted and used by international organizations such as OECD)[47] were developed with extensive input from Nobel Laureate Daniel Kahneman and University of Illinois psychology professor Ed Diener. These metrics stress that 'well-being' is more than just 'happiness', which has been described as too narrow a concept to measure all dimensions of human development (Conceição and Bandura, 2008).

In *Wellbeing: The Five Essential Elements,* Gallup scientists identified career, social connections, personal economics, health and community as the main contributors to a person's overall subjective well-being (Rath and Harter, 2010). Because these elements are interdependent, they must be considered together to reveal a complete picture of migrants' well-being (see figure 11).

---

47 See, for instance, OECD's report How's Life: Measuring Well-being, 2011. Available from www.keepeek.com/Digital-Asset-Management/oecd/economics/how-s-life/subjective-well-being_9789264121164-14-en.

Figure 11   Gallup's essential elements of well-being

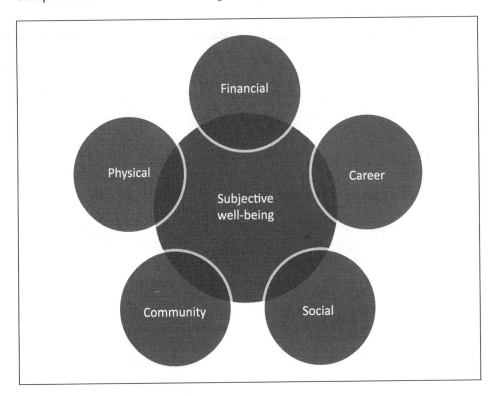

Well-being is about the combination of our love for what we do each day, the quality of our relationships, the security of our finances, the vibrancy of our physical health, and the pride we take in what we have contributed to our communities. Most importantly, it's about how these five elements interact. [...]These are the universal elements of well-being that differentiate a thriving life from one spent suffering (Rath and Harter, 2010).

Subjective well-being

Kahneman distinguishes between two forms of subjective well-being: experiential and evaluative (Kahneman and Riis, 2005). Experiential well-being is, according to Kahneman, concerned with momentary affective states and the way people feel about experiences in real time, while evaluative well-being refers to the way they remember their experiences afterwards.

Evaluative well-being may include individual assessments of life domains such as standard of living, housing, job, marriage, personal health, and other things that matter to a person. Experiential well-being seeks to bypass the effects of judgement and memory to capture feeling and emotions as close to the subject's immediate experience as possible. Deaton et al., have shown that, at the national level, evaluative well-being correlates with income, education and health (Deaton, 2008; Deaton, Fortson and Tortora, 2010), suggesting that this aspect of well-being is an important construct to analyse in the migrant experience (Esipova et al., 2011).

Chapter 4
Dimensions of migrant well-being:
Evidence from the Gallup World Poll   112

Gallup measures 'evaluative well-being' by asking respondents to rate their actual life, overall, and to estimate what their life might be like in five years. Feedback on 'experiential well-being' is obtained by asking respondents about a set of positive and negative feelings that individuals experience during the day.[48]

Financial well-being

Previous Gallup research findings show that people with a high degree of financial well-being are satisfied with their standard of living and are able to achieve a certain level of financial security. Gallup gauges people's personal economic situations and the situations of the communities they live in, using a series of subjective measures that complement more traditional macroeconomic indicators, such as income.

Career well-being

Well-being in one's career is one of the most essential of the five aspects of well-being. Gallup research shows that, without it, the odds of having a high degree of well-being in the other areas decrease. People with a high level of career well-being are more than twice as likely to evaluate their lives at the highest level possible. In this context, Gallup examines individuals' employment status, their views about their own job situation, perceptions of entrepreneurship, and potential obstacles to business creation.

Community well-being

Gallup gauges community well-being by measuring people's perceptions of their personal safety, their confidence in national institutions, their view of the existence of corruption in business and government, their civic engagement, their community attachment, and their perceptions of diversity. People with a high degree of community well-being feel safe and secure where they live and exhibit confidence in their institutions.

Social well-being

People with a high degree of social well-being are surrounded by people who support their development and growth. Gallup assesses migrants' social support structures and their opportunities to make friends in the city or area where they live.

Physical well-being

People with a high level of physical well-being manage their health effectively (Rath and Harter, 2010). In this study, Gallup measures physical well-being worldwide by studying people's perceptions of their own personal health. Gallup also measures their satisfaction with their access to good-quality health care and their likelihood of having health or medical insurance.

---

48   OECD uses our World Gallup Poll data for its measures of subjective well-being at the country level. See: www.keepeek.com/Digital-Asset-Management/oecd/economics/how-s-life/subjective-well-being_9789264121164-14-en.

Subjective well-being: Evaluative and experiential dimensions

Key findings

- North–North migrants rate their current lives as similar to those of the native-born in the countries they live in, and they are even more optimistic about their future. They also report similar levels of positive emotions. By contrast, individuals migrating in other directions (North–South, South–North, South–South) are less likely than the native-born to report feelings of happiness and enjoyment.

- Migrants in the North rate their lives better than do their counterparts in their countries of origin. Migrants in the South rate their lives similar to, or worse than, matched stayers in their home country.

- Migrants who move from South to South feel the worst about their present and future lives. This pessimism is also a common theme in most other aspects of their well-being.

- All migrants – particularly newcomers – are more likely than the native-born to experience sadness.

- While North–North migrants are, overall, on a par with the native-born in host countries, in terms of positive and negative emotions, South–North migrants have a lower prevalence of positive emotions and a higher prevalence of negative emotions. Compared with matched stayers in their home countries, South–North migrants are likely to be better off, in terms of how they rate their current lives.

- South–South long-timers are less likely than newcomers or the native-born to experience positive emotions.

Evaluative well-being: Assessment of one's life today and in the future

North–North migrants fare the best, rating their current lives as similar to those of the native-born in destination countries. South–South migrants fare the worst, in terms of life evaluations. South–North migrants do not rate their lives as highly as the native-born in their current country of residence, but they rate their lives higher than matched stayers. For those migrating from North to South, migration makes no difference, as life ratings are on a par with the people in the country of destination and in the country of birth.

Subjective life evaluations are the cornerstone of well-being and are particularly relevant in the migration dialogue, as research shows that individuals with a high level of subjective well-being are less likely to want to migrate (Cai, Esipova and Oppenheimer, 2012). Gallup measures overall evaluative well-being by asking respondents to rate their current and future lives on a ladder scale (based on the Cantril Self-Anchoring Striving Scale),[49] with steps numbered from 0 to 10. Zero represents the worst possible life and 10 represents the best possible life.

Chapter 4
Dimensions of migrant well-being:
Evidence from the Gallup World Poll

114

49 For details of how Gallup uses the Cantril Scale, see: www.gallup.com/poll/122453/understanding-gallup-uses-cantril-scale.aspx.

Migrants who have moved from North to North are as optimistic about their actual lives as the native-born in their destination countries, and even more optimistic about how they think their lives will be in five years. South–North migrants, however, rate their actual lives significantly lower than the native-born do. But while long-timers are the most pessimistic about their future lives, newcomers are as optimistic about their future lives as the native-born. Long-timers who moved from South to South feel worse about their actual and future lives than those who moved from the North. There is no difference between North–South migrants and the native-born, in terms of how they rate their actual lives, but migrants are more pessimistic about their future (see figure 12).

Figure 12   Ratings of actual and future life, by migrants and the native-born, on the four migration pathways, 2009–2011

Survey questions put to Gallup poll respondents: Please imagine a ladder with steps numbered from 0 at the bottom to 10 at the top. Suppose we say that the top of the ladder represents the best possible life for you, and the bottom of the ladder represents the worst possible life for you. On which step of the ladder would you say you personally feel you stand at this time? On which step do you think you will stand in the future – say about five years from now?

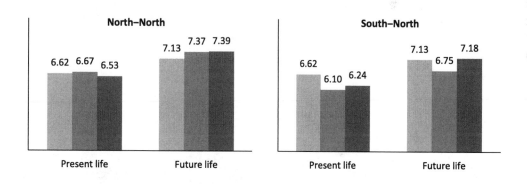

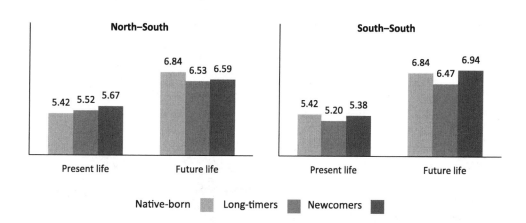

Source: Gallup World Poll, 2009–2011.
Note: Data have been adjusted by age, sex and education.

Are migrants better off for having moved, according to their life evaluations?

Long-timer North–North migrants consider themselves to be better off in their new country, in terms of their actual and future life evaluations, than they would be in their country of origin. Long-timer South–North migrants, however, consider themselves to be currently better off than they would be back home, but they see their future as being no different. South–South long-timers not only consider their actual lives to be worse than the lives of the native-born, but also consider themselves to be worse off than if they'd stayed in their home countries (see figure 13).

 Figure 13   Ratings of actual and future life, by long-timers and matched stayers, on the four migration pathways, 2009–2011

Survey questions put to Gallup poll respondents: Please imagine a ladder with steps numbered from 0 at the bottom to 10 at the top. Suppose we say that the top of the ladder represents the best possible life for you, and the bottom of the ladder represents the worst possible life for you. On which step of the ladder would you say you personally feel you stand at this time? On which step do you think you will stand in the future – say about five years from now?

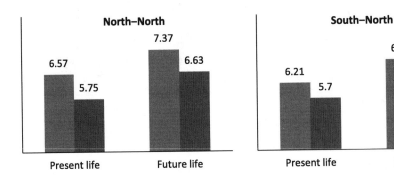

Source: Gallup World Poll, 2009–2011.

Chapter 4
Dimensions of migrant well-being:
Evidence from the Gallup World Poll   116

 **Migrant Voices**

Work and security in the United States: The experience of a Mexican migrant (South–North)

Alfredo has been living in the United States for 26 years. He originally arrived with the intention of working and saving money for two years and then returning to Mexico, as he could earn much more in the United States than was possible at home. However, Alfredo ended up making the United States his home. For the past 21 years, he has been working in a Mexican restaurant and has moved up from busboy, to waiter, to cashier and, most recently, to assistant manager. Finding his job was not difficult as Alfredo had authorization to work. Those who don't have papers are mistreated, he says: "An American might earn USD 8, but someone without papers earns half that." While Alfredo enjoys his work, he loves dancing Zumba and has been offered classes to learn to be a teacher. But he says that, at his age, it is more realistic to remain in his current employment and to continue dancing as a hobby.

Alfredo is financially stable and feels that his situation has improved since leaving Mexico. "In this country, there is a lot," he remarks. Alfredo has many friends from the United States, Mexico and the Philippines, among others. He and his wife live in a small and peaceful neighbourhood, close to nature and animals. "Here, you see squirrels, raccoons, deer," he says, and the city where they live is small, with just 55,000 inhabitants. He says the neighbourhood is safe, and that neighbours watch out for each other. Alfredo appreciates how helpful and supportive members of the community are. "The other day, [my neighbour] helped me to cut down a tree with his power saw," he says. "When I go for vacation, my neighbours offer to care for my property and my lawn, which is very big. I love my community and have made good friendships."

Alfredo feels safer with American police and with the justice system. Alfredo ranks his health a 7 or 8 out of 10. While he is offered health insurance through his employer after paying a percentage, Alfredo prefers not to enroll in this as he is diabetic and says the cost would be high. Although he pays a lot to see the doctor, he is very well attended to.

Alfredo is happy with his decision to move to the United States and is satisfied with his life. What he appreciates most is his family and his way of life: "Here, if you work hard and persevere, in a short time, you can have a dignified way of life, a good house; I have three cars, a job... In Mexico, people work hard to eat; the poor get poorer and the rich get richer." What he finds the most difficult in the United States is the inequality and racism, although he notes that Latinos are increasingly gaining important positions and believes that their "time will come" and that these problems will be resolved. Alfredo is hopeful about the future of Latinos in the United States and about his own life. When asked about the future, he thinks of his granddaughters and his son who will soon be entering university. He hopes to be working so he can finance his son's studies and continue to provide for his family.

Experiential well-being: Positive or negative experiences

North–North migrants are on a par with the native-born in destination countries, when it comes to experiencing positive feelings during the day, whereas other categories of migrants (particularly those who have moved South–South) are less likely than the native-born to report having positive emotions.

Subjective well-being involves a 'multidimensional evaluation of life'. According to Diener (2009b), life evaluations can be more cognitive, as in assessing one's satisfaction with life, or they can be more affective, relating to "moods and emotions, which are reactions to what is happening in someone's life". Gallup measures these 'affective' evaluations by asking questions about the positive and negative feelings that individuals experience during the day, such as happiness, enjoyment, stress and anger, thereby capturing an important dimension of the subjective experiences of migrants in their country of residence.

Migrants who have moved from North to North are generally as likely as the native-born to report having felt positive emotions, such as happiness and enjoyment, the day before the survey. North–North migrants, however, are also more likely than the native-born to report feeling sad, with more than one quarter of long-timers (27%) and newcomers (29%) reporting sad feelings, versus less than a fifth (18%) of the native-born. South–North migrants are less likely than the native-born residents to report positive emotions and more likely to report sadness, anger and worry (see figures 14 and 15).

All migrants in the South are less likely than the native-born living there to report positive emotions. South–South long-timers, in particular, are the least likely to be happy and enjoying life, with barely more than half (53%) saying they were happy a lot the day before the survey (see figure 14).

Chapter 4
Dimensions of migrant well-being:
Evidence from the Gallup World Poll 118

Figure 14 Positive feelings experienced during the day by newcomers, long-timers and the native-born, on the four migration pathways, 2009–2011

Survey question put to Gallup poll respondents: Did you experience the following feelings during a lot of the day yesterday?

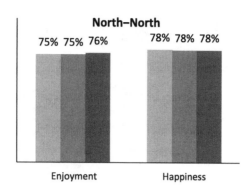

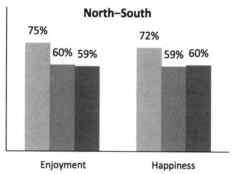

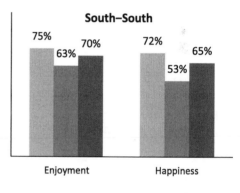

Native-born ▨ Long-timers ▨ Newcomers ▨

Source: Gallup World Poll, 2009–2011.
Notes: 1) Percentages indicate affirmative responses.
2) Data have been adjusted by age, sex and education.

Figure 15   Negative feelings experienced during the day by newcomers, long-timers and the native-born, on the four migration pathways, 2009–2011

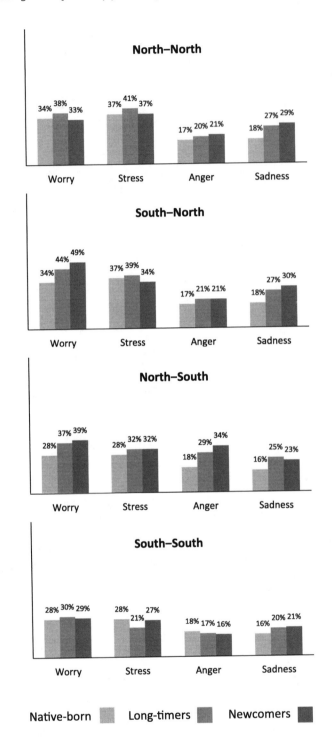

Survey question put to Gallup poll respondents: Did you experience the following feelings during a lot of the day yesterday?

Source: Gallup World Poll, 2009–2011.
Notes: 1) Percentages indicate affirmative responses.
2) Data have been adjusted by age, sex and education.

Chapter 4
Dimensions of migrant well-being:
Evidence from the Gallup World Poll 120

Financial well-being

As noted in chapter 3, traditional economic indicators do not always correlate with an improvement in well-being. A country may develop economically, but satisfaction with living conditions may not improve markedly. The GDP, for instance, is an important measure of economic activity, but an imprecise indicator of individual well-being, including that of migrants. Survey data on individuals' satisfaction with their living standards, for example, help complete the picture with a bottom-up perspective, based on individual judgement.

Gallup gauges people's financial well-being by measuring their personal economic situations and the situations of the communities in which they live. Indicators of subjective well-being include the degree of satisfaction with living standards and assessments of local economic conditions, while objective indicators include levels of household income and people's ability to afford food and adequate shelter for themselves and their families. The subjective measurements of financial well-being are important complements to objective macroeconomic indicators, particularly when these data are difficult to obtain.

Key findings

- Migrants' financial situations in the North are worse than those of the native-born, but their situations improve with time. Long-term North–North migrants, however, achieve the same levels of financial well-being as the native-born.

- South–South migrants are less well off, financially, than the native-born, and their expectations do not improve with time. For example, long-timers are half as likely to say that their standard of living is getting better (32%) than the native-born (55 %).

- Compared with what their situations would have been like if they had remained in their country of origin, North–North migrants gain in terms of objective and subjective economic indicators. South–South migrants, by contrast, appear to lose out relative to matched stayers, with long-timers being less able to afford housing.

- North–North migrants are less likely than South–North migrants to be struggling to meet their basic needs. South–North migrants also experience less improvement, over time, than North–North migrants.

- While migrants in the South are better able to afford food after being in the country more than five years, there is no such improvement with regard to shelter. In fact, they find it more difficult to afford shelter, compared with matched stayers in their home countries.

Household income

Long-term North–North migrants do best, in terms of household income, and are as likely to form part of the richest section of society as native-born populations in destination countries. By contrast, those who have moved from South to North face the most challenges and are likely to be relatively poor, compared to the native-born population in the destination country. Those who have moved within the South are on the same level as the native-born, whereas newcomers who have moved North–South find themselves relatively better off.

Gallup collects self-reported household income figures from each respondent and assigns each respondent to one of the five income categories, based on the respondent's position in the income distribution of the country. Gallup divides each country sample into quintiles by annual household income. This measure of income indicates how well a person is doing financially in comparison with other people in the country where he or she currently lives. This is particularly interesting to track among newcomers and long-timers, many of whom were likely to have been motivated to move by the prospect of higher incomes (Bartram, 2011).

Overall, migrants who have moved from North to North rate themselves better off financially than migrants who have moved from South to North. In fact, long-term North–North migrants are the only migrant group in the North to be as likely as the native-born to be in the richest quintile of the income distribution – more than 1 in 6 in each group falls into this income category. But the data suggest that newcomers are not as well off, with only about 1 in 10 counted among the richest 20 per cent in the country.

The situation is very different for migrants who have moved from South to North – generally, from middle-income countries to high-income countries, rather than from low-income to high-income countries (Bakewell, 2009). Between 31 per cent and 35 per cent of migrants are in the poorest quintile of the income distribution, making them nearly twice as likely as the native-born (18%) to be in this quintile. Long-term South–North migrants are only slightly better off than newcomers but, again, while their income is moving in the right direction, the data suggest it is improving more slowly than it is for their North–North counterparts (see figure 16).

These types of income-level disparities do not exist in the South, except among migrants who have moved from North to South. Newcomers who move from North to South are best off: roughly one in three are in the richest quintile of the income distribution. This result might reflect, as noted earlier, the increase in retirement migration, return migration, or skilled outmigration from the North to the South, in recent years (see chapter 2).

South–South migrants and the native-born are statistically as likely to fall into the poorest quintile of the income distribution, and the pattern is similar for the richest 20 per cent, reflecting existing research from Ratha and Shaw (2007) that shows most migrants from lower-income countries going to countries with incomes only slightly higher than those in their home country.

Chapter 4
Dimensions of migrant well-being:
Evidence from the Gallup World Poll 122

Figure 16   Household income levels among newcomers, long-timers and the native-born, on the four migration pathways, 2009–2011

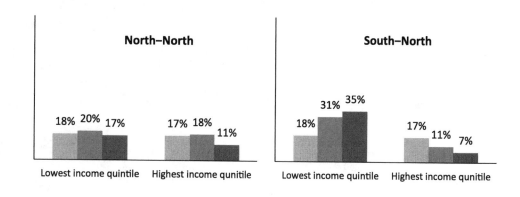

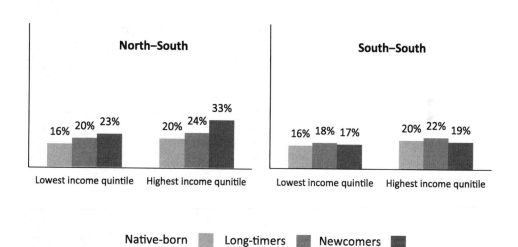

Source: Gallup World Poll, 2009–2011.
Notes: 1) Data have been adjusted by age, sex and education.
2) Quintiles are based on reported household income and calculated within country.

Trading across borders: A trader in the border town of Chirundu, Zambia (South–South)

Raised in a rural village of Zimbabwe, Irene found herself divorced and the mother of three by the age of 28. With little education and with parents who were unable to help her financially, Irene begin her own business trading goods across the border – first in Botswana and later in Zambia. Irene was one of thousands of Zimbabwean women who turned to cross-border trading in the late 1990s as Zimbabwe's economy and standard of living declined.

After one year of trading between Botswana and Zimbabwe, Irene began travelling to neighbouring Zambia. Instead of selling low-value goods to her increasingly impoverished countrymen, as she had before, Irene bought a product in Zimbabwe that Zambians craved – alcohol – and sold it over the border. High duty charges prompted Irene and her business partner to smuggle the goods, with the help of truck drivers. Irene says that most drivers asked to be paid in cash and, while she says she never experienced this herself, she admits that some did ask women for sex in return for their help.

Once in Lusaka, Zambia, Irene sold her goods at the marketplace. With the money she made, she bought US dollars and items to sell once she returned home. With this strategy, Irene managed to make a fairly good living. As she reflected: "The business was good for me: I managed to buy food and take my children to school."

The advent of the Unity Government and the scrapping of the local currency in Zimbabwe in early 2009, however, forced Irene to change the way she operated her business. Many goods, including alcohol, suddenly became more expensive in Zimbabwe than in Zambia, while the black

Chapter 4
Dimensions of migrant well-being:
Evidence from the Gallup World Poll 124

market disappeared overnight and accessing US dollars became very difficult. Now, although Irene continues trading (in goods other than alcohol), she must supplement this income by doing piecework for two or three months with each trip she takes to Chirundu – a border town in Zambia. Taking advantage of the hundreds of truckers clustered around the border for days at a time, Irene offers services such as cooking, gathering firewood and washing clothes. The major unspoken service offered by a number (if not all) of these women involves sex. It would appear that the niche they have carved out for themselves is that of roadside wives. Irene recounts tales of physical abuse for refusing to perform services on credit or for refusing sex. Furthermore, Irene says that the police know that the women are foreigners and they take advantage of their vulnerable position. Consequently, instead of sleeping at the marketplace or under a tree near the road, as she did initially, Irene now rents a shack with other women.

The livelihood strategies adopted by Irene and other Zimbabwean women doing similar work clearly have the potential to adversely affect their health – particularly through exposure to HIV (human immunodeficiency virus) and other sexually transmitted infections, as well as gender-based violence. Other health problems, such as malaria, diarrhoea and cholera, are brought about by the inhospitable environment and the unsanitary living conditions experienced by most.

When asked if she would like her daughters to become cross-border traders, Irene replies without hesitation: "No, they are still young, it's good for them to finish their education so that when they grow up they won't need to be cross-borders – that is not good work... they would start copying bad things from their friends, especially prostitution."

Note: Adapted from Trading across borders, the story of Irene from the Chirundu Border Town, Zambia. In: *Migrant Stories from Southern Africa* (IOM Pretoria, forthcoming).

Food and shelter

All newcomer migrants report difficulties in meeting their basic needs, relative to the native-born in destination countries. Over time, this evens out for North–North migrants, who are likely to be better off than if they'd stayed at home. South–North migrants, however, do not fare nearly as well and their situations do not improve nearly as fast. Migrants from the South are as likely, if not more so, to struggle to afford food and shelter than if they'd stayed at home, especially if they migrate to other countries in the South.

Gallup assesses people's capabilities to meet their basic needs by asking whether there were times in the previous year that they struggled to afford food or adequate shelter for their families. These two measures, taken together, are a good indicator of the prevalence of poverty among migrants – a measure that is not captured at the global level in any other existing surveys. These measures provide additional information about how financial problems affect the individual, in a way that a relative income measure alone cannot. The cost of living can vary significantly within each country, depending on where people live. In one area, a given household income may not even cover basic needs while, in another area, enabling people to live comfortably.

Overall, North–North migrants are less likely than South–North migrants to have problems meeting their food and shelter needs. and, as with their income situations, their ability to meet their basic needs improves with time. North–North long-timers are, therefore, better off than newcomers, and their ability to afford food and shelter rivals that of the native-born. That said, many North–North migrants still experience hardship (see figure 17).

South–North migrants do not fare nearly as well, and their situations do not improve nearly as fast. Newcomers struggle most to meet their basic needs and are at least twice as likely as the native-born in destination countries to say that, at times, in the previous year, they did not have enough money to buy the food they needed (28% for newcomers and 11% for native-born) or adequate shelter (19% and 8%, respectively). Long-term South–North migrants are just as likely as matched stayers in their home country to struggle to meet their basic needs (see figure 18).

South–South newcomers and long-timers are equally likely to struggle to meet their basic needs, with more than 25 per cent struggling with both food and shelter. South–South migrants are more likely than the native-born in the destination country to not have enough money for food and shelter. Finally, North–South migrants, like the native-born in destination countries, struggle to afford food and shelter, and newcomers are most likely to say they did not have enough money for food in the previous 12 months.

Are migrants better off for having moved, in terms of their ability to afford food and shelter?

Compared with what their situations would have been like if they had remained in their country of origin, North–North long-timers are significantly less likely to say that they struggled to afford food and shelter in the past year. South–North long-timers are as likely as their counterparts back home to say they struggled to provide the basics. South–South long-timers are significantly worse off in terms of being able to afford adequate housing: 27 per cent of migrants struggled to afford shelter in the previous year, versus 19 per cent of their counterparts back home. This may reflect higher housing costs in destination countries (see figure 18).

Chapter 4
Dimensions of migrant well-being:
Evidence from the Gallup World Poll 126

Figure 17 **Ability of migrants and the native-born to meet their basic needs (food and shelter), on the four migration pathways, 2009–2011**

Survey question put to Gallup poll respondents: Have there been times in the past 12 months when you did not have enough money to i) buy food and ii) provide adequate housing for you and your family?

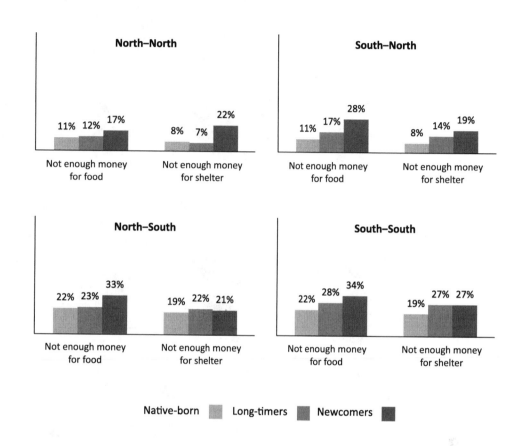

Source: Gallup World Poll, 2009–2011.
Note: Data have been adjusted by age, sex and education.

 **Figure 18** Ability of long-timers and matched stayers to meet their basic needs (food and shelter), on the four migration pathways, 2009–2011

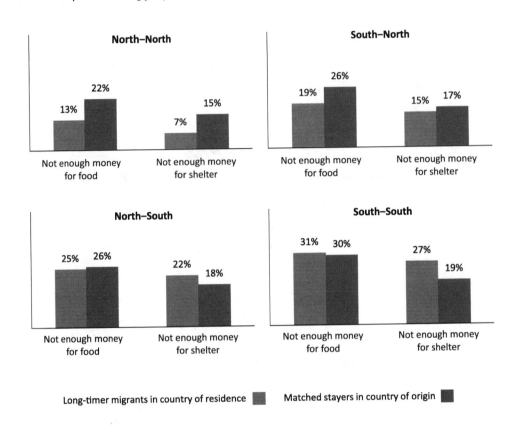

Survey question put to Gallup poll respondents: Have there been times in the past 12 months when you did not have enough money to: i) buy food and ii) provide adequate housing for you and your family?

North–North

13% 22% Not enough money for food
7% 15% Not enough money for shelter

South–North

19% 26% Not enough money for food
15% 17% Not enough money for shelter

North–South

25% 26% Not enough money for food
22% 18% Not enough money for shelter

South–South

31% 30% Not enough money for food
27% 19% Not enough money for shelter

Long-timer migrants in country of residence ▇   Matched stayers in country of origin ▇

Chapter 4
Dimensions of migrant well-being:
Evidence from the Gallup World Poll 128

Living standards

Long-term North–North migrants are as satisfied as the native-born in destination countries with their living standards and are better off for having moved. Migrants from the South have more difficulty in achieving a satisfactory standard of living and do not appear to be better off than if they'd stayed at home.

Gallup also looks at household income in a more subjective way – asking people how they feel about their actual household income and whether they are living comfortably, getting by, finding it difficult, or finding it very difficult to live. In addition, migrants were asked whether they were satisfied with their current situations (namely, with all the things they can buy and do with their money), and whether they envisage their living standards getting better or worse.

With regard to actual household income, the results indicate that migrants originating in the South do not fare as well as the native-born in destination countries. For instance, 12 per cent of South–North migrants find it very difficult to get by on their current incomes (compared to only 6% of the native-born) and fewer of them are living comfortably (see figure 19). Similarly, South–South migrants are also more likely than the native-born to say it is very difficult for them to get by on their current incomes. This outlook only gets bleaker with time. Long-timers are the least likely to be satisfied with their standard of living (44%) and are least likely to say that it is getting better (32%) and that the economic conditions in the local area are good (44%) (see figure 20).

In the North–North context, the situation appears better for both migrants and the native-born. Few people (8% or less, among newcomers, long-timers and the native-born) report that they find it very difficult to get by on their current incomes, and the proportion of people living comfortably is higher than elsewhere (figure 19). Of all migrants, North–North long-timers are best off, in terms of meeting their basic needs, and they are more likely to be satisfied with their standard of living and the economic conditions where they live than are migrants moving in other directions.

However, if compared with the native-born living in the destination country, migrants are less satisfied with their current standard of living, both in the North and the South. Although, in the North, migrants and the native-born share similar optimistic views with regard to the improvement of their living standards and the economic conditions in the destination country, migrants in the South are less optimistic than the native-born living there.

Are migrants better off for having moved, in terms of living standards?

North–North long-timers are not only better off, in terms of meeting their basic needs in their adopted country than they would have been in their country of origin, but also more likely to be satisfied with their standard of living and to believe that economic conditions are good in the city or area where they live. More North–North migrants are "living comfortably" than matched stayers. South–North long-timers are no better off, in terms of meeting their basic needs and satisfaction with their standard of living, than they would have been back home.

Compared with the situation back home, South–South long-timers are worse off in their adopted country, in terms of their ability to afford shelter. Their satisfaction with their standard of living and their outlook for the future are also worse, as are their evaluations of their household income. These findings help us understand why South–South long-timers are less optimistic regarding so many different aspects: based on their perceptions, they have gained little from their lateral move.

Figure 19 **Feelings among migrants and the native-born about household income, on the four migration pathways, 2009–2011**

Survey question put to Gallup poll respondents: Which one of these phrases comes closest to your own feelings about your household's income these days: Living comfortably on present income? Getting by on present income? Finding it difficult on present income? Finding it very difficult on present income?

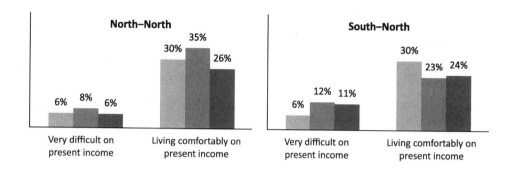

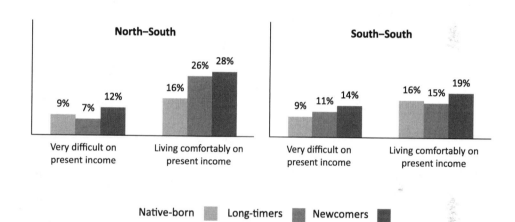

Source: Gallup World Poll, 2009–2011.
Note: Data have been adjusted by age, sex and education.

 Figure 20   Level of satisfaction among migrants and the native-born with their standard of living and local economic conditions, on the four migration pathways, 2009–2011

Survey questions put to Gallup poll respondents: Are you satisfied or dissatisfied with your standard of living, all the things you can buy and do? Right now, do you feel your standard of living is getting better or getting worse? Do you believe the current economic conditions in the city or area where you live are good, or not?

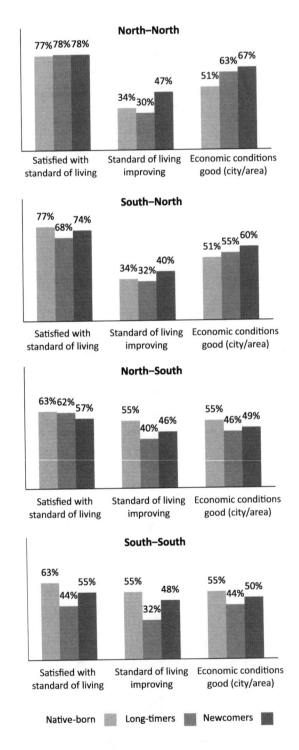

Chapter 4
Dimensions of migrant well-being:
Evidence from the Gallup World Poll   132

Source: Gallup World Poll, 2009–2011.
Note: Data have been adjusted by age, sex and education.

Remittances

Measuring international remittances and the financial help that households receive from individuals in their own countries is vital, not only because these remittances represent lifelines for millions worldwide, but also because they facilitate development. Gallup is able to study both categories, providing a more complete picture of the structure of remittances worldwide that reflects their true magnitude. Previous Gallup findings suggest that about 3 per cent of adults worldwide live in households that receive remittances (in the form of money or goods) from someone in their own country. In many developing countries, however, these figures are much higher. Households worldwide are three times more likely to get financial help from individuals within the same country than from outside the country (Pugliese and Ray, 2011).

Gallup's studies of migrants and the native-born across more than 130 countries provide a closer look at those who are sending this financial help to others. Overall, the native-born in the North and South are more likely to send financial help within their own country than to another country – as might be expected. Migrants in the North and the South, on the other hand, are more likely than the native-born to send financial help to another country.

 Table 13   Percentage of migrants and native-born sending remittances, 2009–2011

	Migrants	Native-born
South		
Send financial help within country	14%	13%
Send financial help to another country	8%	1%
North		
Send financial help within country	21%	27%
Send financial help to another country	27%	7%

Source: Gallup World Poll, 2011–2012.

Career well-being

Well-being in one's career is closely linked to financial well-being and addresses the employment status of individuals, their views about their own job situation, and perceptions of entrepreneurship, including the potential obstacles to setting up a business.

Key points

- Overall, migrants have a higher labour participation rate than the native-born in destination countries (66% versus only 62%, respectively) but the young are more likely to be out of the labour force or unemployed. However, migrants are more likely than the native-born to be unemployed or underemployed, particularly in the North.

- Migrants in the North (63%) are slightly more likely than the native-born (59%) to be part of the workforce, but only half of them work full time for an employer. Migrants in the South (61%) are less likely than the native-born (67%) to be in the labour force, but those in the labour force are doing as well as the native-born, in terms of employment status.

- Migrants in the North are more likely to be underemployed or unemployed than the native-born living there: 26 per cent are underemployed (compared with 18% of the native-born) and 13 per cent are unemployed (versus 8% of the native-born).

- When it comes to the right placement, migrants are less likely than the native-born to feel that their job is "ideal". The only exception is North–South migrants, who are on a par with the native-born.

- Migrants in the North are more likely to have entrepreneurial ambitions than are the native-born living there. This difference is less marked between the native-born and migrants in the South.

- In the North, migrants and the native-born are equally likely to own a business. Among those who do not own a business, migrants are more likely than the native-born to think about, and plan to start, a business in the next 12 months. In the South, migrants are less likely than the native-born to own a business.

- Migrants in the North are more optimistic than the native-born in destination countries regarding nearly all aspects of the business climate. Migrants in the South, however, are least likely to view the climate as business-friendly: for instance, 34 per cent of migrants in the North (versus 27% of the native-born) believe that the government makes it easy to start a business while, in the South, only 22 per cent of migrants feel this way (versus 43% of the native-born).

- In the North, the majority (85%) of businesses are formally registered. In the South, migrants are more likely (55%) than the native-born (42%) to formally register their business.

People's careers shape their identity and well-being. The Gallup global surveys reveal that people with 'good jobs' (defined as those who are formally employed full time by an employer) tend to have the highest well-being of those in the workforce (Clifton and Marlar, 2011). These people are more likely to rate their actual and future lives positively than those who are self-employed, employed part time and looking for full-time work, or unemployed.

Chapter 4
Dimensions of migrant well-being:
Evidence from the Gallup World Poll 134

Box 7

Defining and measuring labour statistics in the Gallup World Poll

Gallup classifies respondents based on their answers to several questions about employment. Among those in the workforce, Gallup's employment metrics allow for a calculation of the percentage of migrants working full time for an employer, the percentage of unemployed, and the percentage of underemployed:

Employed full time by an employer
The 'Gallup Employed Full Time for an Employer Index' measures the percentage of the workforce that is employed full time by an employer. A person is classified as employed by an employer if he or she works at least 30 hours per week for an employer.

Unemployment
The Gallup Unemployment Rate is the percentage of unemployed adults who actively looked for work within the preceding four weeks, and could have begun to work in that time frame. Gallup's unemployment measure is comparable to the Bureau of Labor Statistics (BLS) and the International Labour Organization (ILO) unemployment calculations.

Underemployment
The Gallup Underemployment Index measures the percentage of adults in the workforce who are working at less than the desired capacity. People are classified as 'underemployed' if they are employed part time but want to work full time OR if they are unemployed but want to be working.

Gallup estimates that about 62 per cent of all adults worldwide are in the labour force. These individuals are either currently employed or actively seeking, and able to begin, work. Gallup's Labour Force Participation Rate measures the percentage of the adult population (aged 15 and older) that is in the labour force.

 Table 14   Labour status among migrants and the native-born, 2009–2011

	Migrants	Native-born
Labour force participation rate	66%	62%
Underemployment Index	25%	18%
Unemployment Index	13%	8%

Source: Gallup World Poll, 2009–2011.

Employment status and job satisfaction

Migrants in the North are slightly more likely than the native-born to be part of the workforce, although they are more likely to be underemployed or unemployed. The converse is true in the South, where migrants are less likely than the native-born to be part of the workforce but more likely to work full time for an employer. Migrants generally report being less satisfied with their jobs than do the native-born in destination countries, except for North–South migrants, who report slightly higher levels of satisfaction.

Migrants in the North (63%) are slightly more likely than the native-born living there to be part of the workforce (59%), but migrants are less likely to work full time for an employer (52% and 56%, respectively), and are more likely to be underemployed (26% versus 18%) or unemployed (13% versus 8%). In the South, on the other hand, migrants are less likely than the native-born to be part of the workforce (61% and 67%, respectively), but they are more likely to work full time for an employer (48% versus 44%) and just as likely as the native-born to be underemployed or unemployed (see figure 21).

 Figure 21   **Employment status, rate of participation in labour force and level of job satisfaction among migrants and the native-born, in the North and South, 2009–2011**

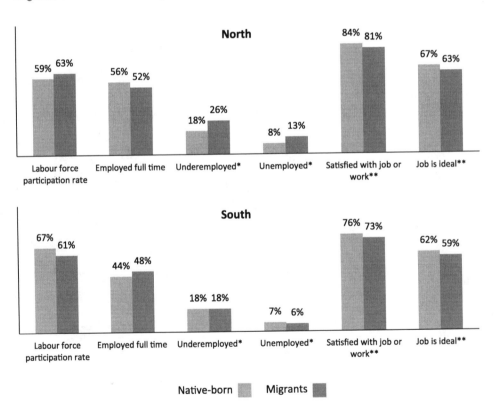

Source: Gallup World Poll, 2009–2011.

Notes: 1) * denotes: among those in the labour force; ** denotes: among those employed.

        2) Data have been adjusted by age, sex and education.

        3) Employment status and rate of participation in labour force are determined as explained in box 7; the level of job satisfaction is determined by asking Gallup poll respondents: *Are you satisfied or dissatisfied with your job or the work you do? Would you say that your job is the ideal job for you, or not?*

Chapter 4
Dimensions of migrant well-being:
Evidence from the Gallup World Poll 136

Similarly, in terms of the four migration pathways, North–North and South–North migrants are less likely than the native-born to work full time for an employer, and more likely than the native-born to be underemployed or unemployed. While North–North migrants are just as likely to be part of the labour force, South–North migrants (66%) are even more likely to participate than the native-born (59%). North–South and South–South migrants are less likely to participate in the labour force than the native-born. Finally, South–South migrants are slightly more likely than the native-born to work full time for an employer.

Figure 22   Employment status and rate of participation in labour force among migrants and the native-born, on the four migration pathways, 2009–2011

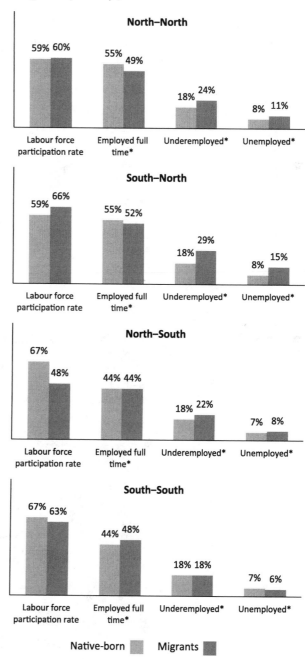

Source: Gallup World Poll, 2009–2011.
Notes: 1) * denotes: among those in labour force.
            2) Data have been adjusted by age, sex and education.

Gallup's definition of underemployment does not address whether migrants are working below their skill or education levels, and migrant workers (who are increasingly arriving in destination countries without jobs (OECD, 2007)) tend to fill vacant jobs, sometimes taking positions for which they are over-qualified, and working in precarious environments (IOM, 2010a).

Although Gallup's data do not address this type of situation directly, they do show that employed North–North migrants are less likely than the native-born to say they are satisfied with their job (75% and 84%, respectively) or to say that their job is the ideal one for them (59% versus 67%), although the majority feel this to be the case. South–North migrants are as likely to be satisfied with their jobs as the native-born, but are less likely than the native-born to say their job is ideal. Employed South–South migrants, on the other hand, are less satisfied with their jobs than the native-born and are less likely to consider their job ideal, while the North–South migrants' job satisfaction is comparable to that of the native-born (see figure 23).

Are migrants more likely to find employment?

Migrants who moved from South to North are more likely to be employed full time by an employer, but they are also more likely to be unemployed or underemployed than are matched stayers in their country of origin. Migrants who moved from South to South, on the other hand, are less likely to be underemployed or unemployed than matched stayers in their country of origin.

 Migrant Voices

Working towards regaining professional identity and status (South–North)

Elena is a woman who is passionate about what she does. Her love of numbers and calculations came from her father, an economist in the capital of the Eurasian country from which she hails. Elena followed his lead by studying economics and finance, and later worked for eight years as an accountant for various companies.

Shortly after Elena's husband started to work for the leading political opposition figure in the country, he went missing. Facing threats and intimidation and fearing for her security and that of her 15-year-old son, Elena decided to leave for Switzerland and to apply for asylum there.

Once in Switzerland, she and her son were offered emergency accommodation, as well as some French language classes. "I was used to working and making my own money, being totally financially independent," she says. "On top of everything else we've been through with leaving our country, ending up dependent on social aid was very

Chapter 4
Dimensions of migrant well-being:
Evidence from the Gallup World Poll 138

difficult." While seeking recognition for her credentials, looking for a job in her profession and learning the language, Elena took a job in a cleaning company to support herself and her son.

Facing refusal after refusal, Elena realized that the qualifications and experience she had obtained in her country of origin were viewed with a great deal of suspicion by employers. This unsuccessful job search took a heavy toll on her morale and psychological well-being. The exhausting and physically demanding job exacerbated the stress of exile from her home and of her husband's disappearance.

In addition, settling for an unfulfilling job resulted not only in a sense of loss of satisfaction with her profession, but also a loss of belonging and identity for Elena. "My profession was what I had wanted to do since I was little – a passion for which I worked a lot, over the years. It is hard to think that all those efforts to study, excel and perfect my skills have come down to nothing," she says.

Now in Switzerland for almost five years, Elena has enrolled in a university programme to regain her professional status as a certified accountant, thanks to support from public authorities. She is also taking a professional English course to adapt her skills to the needs of the local labour market and is hopeful that she will find a job in her field of work.

Note: The name of this respondent has been changed to protect her privacy. She was interviewed during the research phase of IOM's recent publication on the psychosocial impact of underemployment on skilled migrant women. This report examines some of the human and social costs associated with the stiff barriers to skilled employment that migrants face. The report can be found in chapter 3 of Crushed Hopes: Underemployment and deskilling among skilled migrant women, which also includes research from the United Kingdom and Canada (see IOM, 2012). The French version is available under the title: L'impact psychosocial du sous-emploi sur la vie des femmes migrantes qualifiées travaillant à Genève (Suisse).

Figure 23 Job satisfaction among employed migrants and native-born residents, on the four migration pathways, 2009–2011

Survey questions put to Gallup poll respondents: Are you satisfied or dissatisfied with your job or the work you do? Would you say that your job is the ideal job for you, or not?

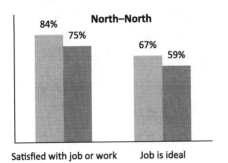

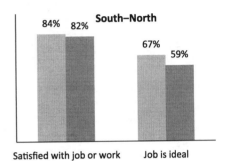

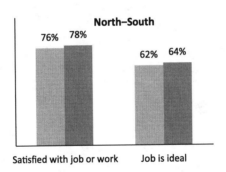

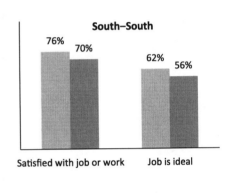

Native-born ▨ Migrants ▨

Source: Gallup World Poll, 2009–2011.
Note: Data have been adjusted by age, sex and education.

Chapter 4
Dimensions of migrant well-being:
Evidence from the Gallup World Poll 140

Entrepreneurship

In the North, migrants are more likely than the native-born to exhibit an entrepreneurial spirit and to show an interest in establishing a business. Migrants in the South are just as interested in establishing a business but are least likely to see the business climate as friendly.

Migrants in many countries are more likely to be self-employed than the native-born living there – perhaps because it offers a way to escape marginalization in the labour market and is an attractive alternative to unemployment (OECD, 2010c). But Gallup's research suggests that some migrants (who are, by their nature, more likely to be risk-takers) may be born entrepreneurs. Gallup defines an entrepreneur as: "an individual who proactively seeks to generate value through expansion of economic activity and who creatively responds to challenges and needs encountered in the process of accomplishing this outcome" (Badal, 2010).

Three factors differentiate people with entrepreneurial spirit from the rest: they feel optimistic, even when things go wrong; they never give up; and they are willing to take a risk. In the North, migrants[50] are more likely than the native-born to exhibit all three characteristics, so it appears that the North attracts more migrants with entrepreneurial inclinations. In the South, there is less difference between migrants and native-born residents than in the North. Migrants and the native-born in the South are as likely to say they never give up and are willing to take a risk, while migrants are more likely to feel optimistic when things go wrong (see figure 24).

50 Because of small sample sizes of business owners and aspiring entrepreneurs, Gallup combines both newcomers and long-timers together in this analysis.

 **Figure 24** Degree of entrepreneurial spirit among migrants and the native-born, in the North and South, 2009–2011

Survey question put to Gallup poll respondents: Please tell me whether you agree or disagree with the following statements: Even when things go wrong, you feel very optimistic. You never give up until you reach your goals, no matter what. You would rather take a risk and build your own business than work for someone else.

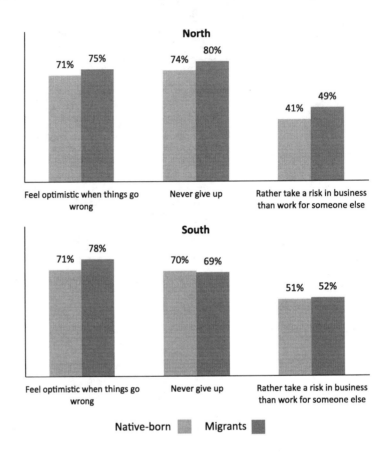

Source: Gallup World Poll, 2009–2011.
Note: Data have been adjusted by age, sex and education.

In the North, the native-born and migrants are as likely to own their own business. At the same time, among those who are not already business owners, migrants are more likely than the native-born to have thought about starting a business (54% and 47%, respectively) and as likely to be planning to start one in the next 12 months (see figure 25). In the South, migrants are slightly less likely than the native-born to own a business but, at the same time, among non-business owners, migrants are as likely as the native-born to consider starting, and plan to start, a business. These findings are consistent with the level of entrepreneurial spirit; in the North, more migrants demonstrated an entrepreneurial spirit than did the native-born.

The conversion rate – from thinking about starting a business to actually planning to start a business – is higher for migrants and the native-born in the South than in the North. This could be because more residents in the South start businesses when they cannot find suitable jobs. In fact, business owners in the South are more likely than those in the North to say they could not find a suitable job.

Chapter 4
Dimensions of migrant well-being:
Evidence from the Gallup World Poll 142

The data raise some interesting questions, such as why migrants in the North, who are more likely to show entrepreneurial spirit than the native-born, are not more likely to own a business, and why migrants in the South, who show the same level of entrepreneurial spirit as the native-born, are less likely to own a business. The data offer some clues. In the North, migrants are less likely than the native-born to know someone who could share the risk of starting a business. In the South, migrants are more likely to perceive obstacles in the business climate.

Figure 25 **Business owners and entrepreneurial intentions among migrants and the native-born in the North and South, 2009–2011**

Survey questions put to Gallup poll respondents: Do you currently own a business? Have you ever thought about starting your own business? Are you planning to start your own business in the next 12 months, or not?

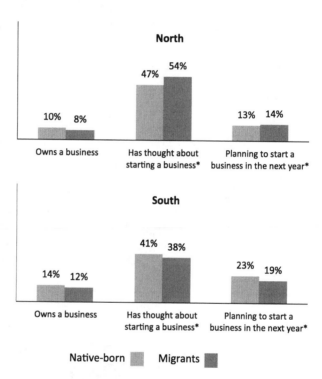

Source: Gallup World Poll, 2009–2011.
Notes: 1) * denotes: among non-business owners.
           2) Data have been adjusted by age, sex and education.

Gallup also asks migrants who are not business owners whether they have the access to training and money that they need to start a business. In the North, migrants say they are less likely to have access to training, but have the same access to money as the native-born. In the South, the situation is reversed; migrants are less likely to have access to money, but have the same access to training.

All migrants in the North are more optimistic than the native-born regarding nearly all aspects of the business climate: they consider doing paperwork/obtaining permits to be easy; they trust assets and property to be safe; and they say that the government makes it easy to start and manage a business. They are, however, less likely to know someone with whom they could go into business, which may be a particular obstacle for migrants who are unfamiliar with the business practices, traditions and culture in their adopted country. On the other hand, migrants in the South are less likely than the native-born to view the climate as business-friendly; for example, only 22 per cent of migrants believe that the government makes it easy to start a business and 17 per cent of migrants believe that the government makes it easy to manage a business (compared with 43% and 37%, respectively, of the native-born living there) (see figure 26).

Figure 26   Perceptions of the business climate among migrants and the native-born in the North and South, 2009–2011

Survey questions put to Gallup poll respondents: In general, does the government make paperwork and permits easy enough for anyone who wants to start a business, or not? If someone wants to start a business, can they trust their assets and property to be safe at all times? Does the government make it easy or hard to start a business? Does the government make it easy or hard to manage a business?

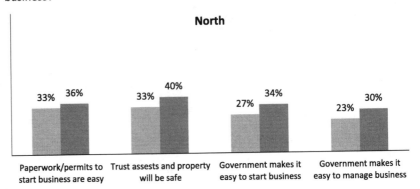

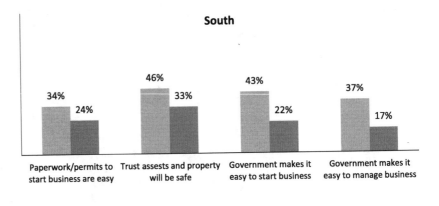

Source: Gallup World Poll, 2009–2011.
Note: Data have been adjusted by age, sex and education.

Are migrants more likely to find a better business climate?

Long-timers in the South are more likely to perceive more challenges in the business climate in their country of residence, compared with matched stayers in their country of origin.

Chapter 4
Dimensions of migrant well-being:
Evidence from the Gallup World Poll   144

The majority of businesses (85%) in the North (owned by the native-born and migrants) are formally registered. In the South, a much lower percentage of businesses are formally registered, and migrants are more likely (55%) than the native-born (42%) to formally register their business. In the North, the native-born and migrants are equally likely to be sole owners but, in the South, migrants are less likely than the native-born to be sole owners. This is probably because migrants in the South have less access to money (see figure 27).

While governments cannot infuse people with an entrepreneurial spirit, they can create conditions that make it easier for those with entrepreneurial aspirations to start a business. They can, for example, make it easier for people to access training, mentors and start-up funds. Other Gallup research shows that social capital is important at every stage of entrepreneurship, but particularly in the start-up phase. Adults who have access to a mentor are three times more likely to say they are planning to start a business (14%) than those who do not have a mentor (5%) (Badal and Srinivasan, 2011). Governments can also remove obstacles, either real or perceived, that make rules and regulations seem less than business-friendly. Networks that connect potential migrant entrepreneurs with successful native-born entrepreneurs would also be beneficial because the latter are likely to have access to social and financial support and may be willing to share some of the risks involved in setting up a business.

Figure 27   **Type of business ownership among migrants and the native-born in the North and South, 2009–2011**

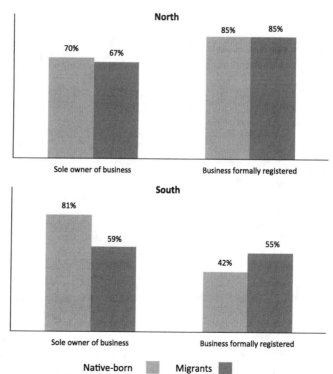

Survey questions put to Gallup poll respondents: Are you the sole owner of this business or do you have partners? Have you formally registered your business, or not?

Source: Gallup World Poll, 2009–2011.
Note: Data have been adjusted by age, sex and education.

Community well-being

People with a high degree of community well-being not only feel safe and secure where they live, but also feel attached to their communities. This often results in their wanting to give back to their community, which, in turn, may actually promote acceptance and inclusiveness in that community. Social relationships and participation in community life are important determinants of the extent to which individuals feel part of the broader community where they live (Boarini et al., 2006).

Gallup gauges community well-being by measuring people's perceptions of their personal safety, their confidence in national institutions, their view of the existence of corruption in business and government, their civic engagement, their community attachment, and their perceptions of diversity.

Key findings

- Migrants in the South are less likely to feel safe in the area where they live than the native-born living there, while migrants in the North feel as safe as native-born residents.
- South–South newcomers are in the most vulnerable situation, in terms of safety: they are least likely to feel safe and most likely to have been mugged or had property stolen.
- Migrants in the North are generally more confident in the institutions in their destination country than the native-born living there. With a few exceptions, migrants in the South either have as much or less confidence in the institutions as the native-born in destination countries.
- Migrants in the North are as likely as the native-born in destination countries to feel that their local leadership represents their interests while, in the South, migrants are less likely to feel this way.
- Relative to all groups in the North, all people in the South are more likely to see corruption as widespread where they live and to have encountered bribery in the previous year.
- Newcomers in the North and South are more likely than the native-born to perceive their local communities as good places to live for immigrants and racial/ethnic minorities. The expectations of long-timers are lower and closer to those of the native-born in countries of destination.

Personal safety

Migrants are generally less secure than the native-born in countries of destination; the situation is particularly pronounced among migrants in the South, who report more incidences of theft or assault than the native-born residents. South–South migrants appear to fare the worst.

Gallup gauges people's sense of personal security by asking them about their general feelings of safety walking alone at night in their communities, and whether they have personally been victims of theft or assault in the past year. The strong relationships that Gallup sees between people's answers to these questions and external measures related to economic and social development (such as per capita GDP, life expectancy and corruption) reinforce additional data confirming that high crime rates suppress social cohesion at the community level

Chapter 4
Dimensions of migrant well-being:
Evidence from the Gallup World Poll

146

(Ayers, 1998) and can negatively affect regional economic performance (Entorf and Spengler, 2000).

For migrants, fear and higher crime victimization rates form real barriers to their full social and economic participation in their adopted country. Gallup's findings show that these barriers are likely to be higher for newcomers, particularly those from the South, who feel the least safe and are the most likely to be victimized. However, the data also show that these barriers eventually do start to come down the longer the migrants stay in their new country.

In the North, the majority of respondents report feeling safe walking alone at night (63% or more, for each category). Newcomers from the South generally feel less safe than newcomers from the North. However, when migrants stay longer than five years in their country of destination, this difference largely disappears.

All migrants in the North are at least as likely, if not more likely, than the native-born living there to have been assaulted or had their property stolen. The relationship between migrant status and burglary or personal theft is also documented in an analysis of British Crime Survey victimization data from 2007/2008, which found that migrants in England and Wales were slightly more at risk than natives of being victims of these types of crimes (Papadopoulos, 2012). The author of the analysis concluded that these higher risks are largely explained by migrants being more likely than natives to live in urban and deprived areas where these types of crimes are more likely to occur.

The situation for migrants in the South is wholly different. South–South newcomers are twice as likely as native-born residents to have been mugged (13% and 6%, respectively) and are also more likely to have had property stolen (23% versus 15%). Long-timers and the native-born are equally likely to have been the victims of these types of crime. The results for North–South newcomers trend in the same direction but, due to smaller sample sizes, the differences are not statistically significant. Given the greater likelihood of their being victims of personal crime, it is not surprising that migrants in the South – especially newcomers – are less likely to feel safe walking alone at night in the area where they live. Overall, South–South newcomers are in the most vulnerable position, in terms of safety, with less than half (44%) saying they feel safe walking alone at night (see figure 28). Some of this insecurity may reflect newcomers' unfamiliarity with their new surroundings, but it may also reflect new migrants' historical tendency to initially live in urban areas that have higher poverty and crime rates.

Are migrants better off for having moved, in terms of personal safety?

The security situation is relatively better for long-timers from South to North, compared with what their experience would have been back at home: they are more likely to say they feel safe walking alone at night. Although the situation is slightly better for long-timers who have moved from South to South, safety is still a significant problem for this group, and their sense of personal safety is less than if they had remained in their home country.

Figure 28 Perceptions of security and incidence of theft/assault among migrants and the native-born, on the four migration pathways, 2009–2011

Survey questions put to Gallup poll respondents: Do you feel safe walking alone at night in the city or area where you live? Within the past 12 months, have you had money or property stolen from you or another household member? Within the past 12 months, have you been assaulted or mugged?

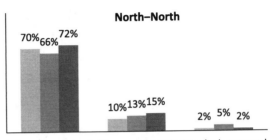

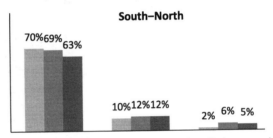

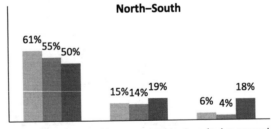

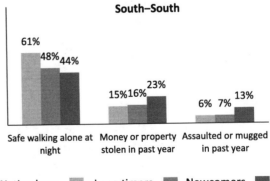

Chapter 4
Dimensions of migrant well-being:
Evidence from the Gallup World Poll 148

Source: Gallup World Poll, 2009–2011.
Note: Data have been adjusted by age, sex and education.

Confidence in national institutions

Migrants in the North are as confident as, or more confident than, the native-born population in the national institutions of the destination country; this is not the case, however, for migrants to the South. South–North migrants tend to have more confidence in national institutions than they would have had in the institutions at home, but South–South migrants have less confidence.

People's confidence in their country's institutions provides insight into how well residents think their government is fulfilling its end of the social contract and representing the people's interests, rather than its own. Broader Gallup research (2012) finds particularly strong relationships between people's confidence in their institutions (such as their national government, their judicial system, and the honesty of their elections) and the aspects of their lives for which they hold these institutions responsible. Confidence is greater when residents have a stronger sense of security, perceive less corruption in government and business, and have a high degree of financial well-being.

Newcomers in the North tend to fully embrace – rather than reject – their new country's institutions. The majority of these migrants, regardless of whether their move has been North to North or South to North, express confidence in nearly all institutions measured (see figures 29 and 30). The rose-coloured glasses come off for long-timers, however, who express less confidence than newcomers but still more than the native-born residents.

Migrants in the South do not have the same confidence in the institutions of their destination country as migrants in the North. With a few exceptions, they either have as much or less confidence than the native-born residents. Migrants who have moved from North to South, particularly, are far more pessimistic about institutions, which makes sense, given the changes one is likely to experience when moving from a developed country to a developing one; for instance, the native-born in the South (61%) are far more likely than newcomers (30%) to approve of the leader of the country. Among South–South migrants, long-timers are the least confident in institutions (see figures 29 and 30).

Do migrants have more confidence in the national institutions of their destination country than they would have had in the institutions of their home country?

South–North long-timers have more confidence in the police, the judicial system, and the electoral process than they would have had in these same institutions back home. From the long-timers' perspective, they moved to countries with better governance than the ones they left. Again, the situation for South–South migrants is perceived as much worse in their adopted country than in their home country – and this is reflected in their greater sense of personal insecurity. Long-timers, in particular, have less confidence in the local police and the judicial system in their destination country than they do back home.

Figure 29   Level of confidence in national government, leadership and electoral system, among migrants and the native-born, on the four migration pathways, 2009–2011

Survey questions put to Gallup poll respondents: In [country name], do you have confidence in each of the following, or not? How about national government? How about honesty of elections? Do you approve or disapprove of the job performance of [country leader]?

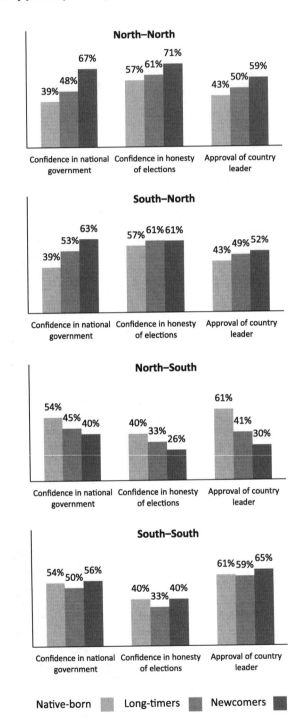

Source: Gallup World Poll, 2009–2011.

Notes: 1) Percentages indicate affirmative responses.
2) Data have been adjusted by age, sex and education.

Chapter 4
Dimensions of migrant well-being: 150
Evidence from the Gallup World Poll

Figure 30 Level of confidence in the police, the judicial system/courts and financial institutions, among migrants and the native-born, on the four migration pathways, 2009–2011

Survey question put to Gallup poll respondents: In [country name], do you have confidence in each of the following, or not?

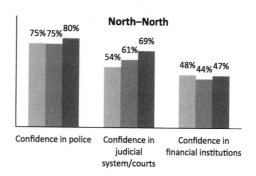

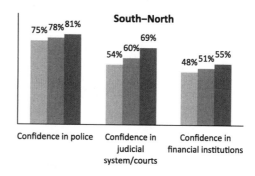

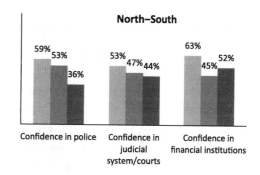

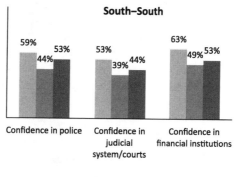

Native-born | Long-timers | Newcomers

Source: Gallup World Poll, 2009–2011.
Notes: 1) Percentages indicate affirmative responses.
            2) Data have been adjusted by age, sex and education.

Corruption

Migrants in the North are less likely than the native-born to believe that corruption is widespread in business and government. Migrants in the South are more likely to see corruption as widespread and to face bribery in their everyday lives.

Gallup (2012) typically finds that the belief that corruption is widespread in business and government translates into lower confidence in national institutions and in law and order, as well as less satisfaction with community infrastructure. Furthermore, the belief that corruption is pervasive has a negative impact on external measures such as the GDP, per capita health expenditures, public resources dedicated to the education system, and the United Nations Human Development Index.

Migrants in the North are less likely than the native-born residents to believe that corruption is widespread in business and government. In addition, although the majority do not believe their governments are doing enough to fight corruption, migrants (44%) are more likely than the native-born (30%) to believe that sufficient effort is being made. This is particularly true for South–North newcomers, 53 per cent of whom believe that their destination country is doing enough. At the same time, migrants in the North are more likely than the native-born to personally encounter bribery, regardless of whether they paid a bribe or not (see figure 31).

Relative to all groups in the North, all groups in the South are more likely to see corruption as widespread where they live and to have encountered bribery in the previous year (figure 31). This is particularly true for long-term South–South migrants, who are even more likely than native-born residents to perceive corruption as widespread in business (75%) and government (76%) and are less likely to believe the government is doing enough about it (23%).

> **Do migrants' views on corruption in their destination country differ from their views on corruption in their home country?**
>
> Long-term South–North migrants report less corruption in their new country than do matched stayers in their home country. This probably helps explain why migrants are more positive than the native-born about the corruption situation. Long-term South–South migrants are more likely to believe that corruption is more widespread in their adopted country than in their country of origin and that the government is not doing enough to fight it. Furthermore, a Gallup analysis on what drives adults to permanently migrate suggests that corruption back home may have been a factor – particularly for those moving from North to North. Widespread corruption in businesses has been shown to drive people to countries with very high human development (Gravelle et al., 2010).

Chapter 4
Dimensions of migrant well-being:
Evidence from the Gallup World Poll 152

Figure 31   Perceptions relating to the level of corruption, the degree of satisfaction with government interventions, and personal experience with bribery, among migrants and the native-born in the North and South, 2009–2011

Survey questions put to Gallup poll respondents: Is corruption widespread within businesses located in [country], or not? Is corruption widespread throughout the government in [country], or not? Do you think the government of your country is doing enough to fight corruption, or not? Sometimes people have to give a bribe or a present in order to solve their problems. In the last 12 months, were you, personally, faced with this kind of situation, or not (regardless of whether you gave a bribe/present or not)?

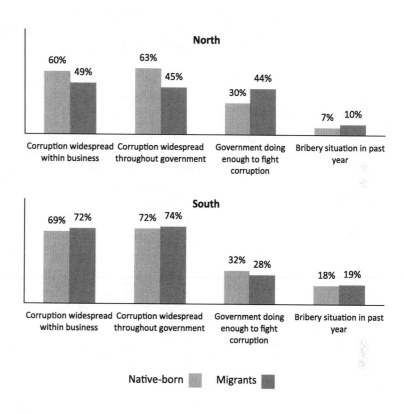

Source: Gallup World Poll, 2009–2011.
Notes: 1) Percentages indicate affirmative responses.
            2) Data have been adjusted by age, sex and education.

Community attachment and diversity

Migrants to all destinations are more likely than the native-born to see the areas where they live as being good places for racial minorities or immigrants to live in. Migrants to the North are as satisfied as the native-born in destination countries with the communities they live in, whereas migrants in the South feel less attachment.

Gallup measures people's attachment to their communities by studying their satisfaction with the city or area in which they live and the likelihood of them moving away or of recommending the city or area to a friend as a place to live. This community attachment is important because it affects whether a community attracts and retains talented people whose skills and knowledge can create new business and jobs that help improve the economy.

In the North, migrants and the native-born residents all report high satisfaction with their communities as places to live, would recommend their communities to others, and feel that their local leadership represents their interests. In the South, on the other hand, migrants feel less attachment: they are less likely than the native-born to say their local leadership acts in their interests (in line with their attitudes towards national leadership), and less likely to say their communities are the ideal places for them to live (see figure 32).

Gallup also measures whether people consider their communities to be good places to live for people from other specific backgrounds – such as racial minorities and immigrants. In the North and South, migrants are more likely than the native-born residents to perceive the area where they currently live as good places for racial minorities or immigrants to live. On each of the four migration pathways, newcomers are most enthusiastic, initially, although their enthusiasm diminishes, over time.

Chapter 4
Dimensions of migrant well-being:
Evidence from the Gallup World Poll 154

Figure 32 Degree of community attachment among migrants and the native-born, in the North and South, 2009–2011

Survey question put to Gallup poll respondents: Please tell me whether you agree or disagree with the following statements: Leaders in the city or area where you live represent your interests. You would recommend the city or area where you live to a friend or associate as a place to live. Your city or area is the ideal place for you to live.

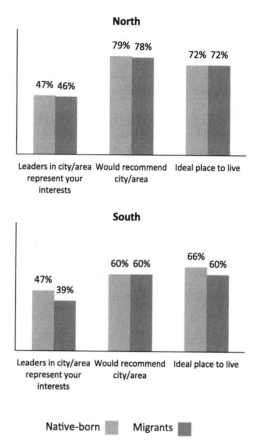

Source: Gallup World Poll, 2009–2011.
Notes: 1) Percentages indicate affirmative responses.
   2) Data have been adjusted by age, sex and education.

Social well-being

Broader Gallup research reveals that people with a high level of social well-being are surrounded by people who encourage their development and growth (Rath and Harter, 2010). These people spend time investing in their social networks. The aspects of social well-being that Gallup measures relate to the respondents' social support structure and their opportunities to make friends in the city/area where they live – key assets for all migrants when they join a community.

Key findings

- North–North and South–South migrants are as well connected socially as native-born residents, and they are as well connected as they would have been in their home country. Migrants who moved from a developing country to a developed country, or vice versa, report fewer social connections and need help building a support network in their new country.

- Newcomers are more likely than long-timers to have someone living in another country that they can depend on. Long-timers may have lost their connections back home or perhaps more family and friends have joined them in the destination country. In any case, both migrant groups have more connections abroad than do the native-born in the destination country.

Social networks

Migrants moving North–North or South–South have established social networks on a par with the native-born. By contrast, migrants moving between the North and South, in either direction, report having fewer social contacts.

In the North–North context, migrants have established social networks that are more or less on a par with the support structures of the native-born. Newcomers, long-timers and the native born are all equally likely to report having someone in their lives that they can count on and all are equally satisfied with opportunities to meet new friends (approximately 80% in each group are satisfied). Similarly, South–South migrants' social connections are generally on a par with those of the native-born residents. They are just as likely as the native-born to be satisfied with opportunities to meet new people and to have someone to count on. South–South migrants are generally more likely than the native-born to spend more time (more than five hours a day, on average) with friends and family, while the number of friends that they talk to (every two weeks) is the same as for the native-born (see figures 33 and 34).

The situation for South–North migrants is very different. The native-born are more likely than the migrants to have someone they can count on; they spend more hours with friends; and they talk to more friends. Accordingly, South–North migrants are less likely to be satisfied with opportunities to meet people and make friends and, it appears, their situations do not improve with time: long-timers (82%) are no more likely than newcomers (84%) to report having friends or relatives on whom they can depend.

Are migrants more likely to improve their social networks?

Long-timers who have moved from South to North appear to lose more of their social networks than do matched stayers in their country of origin. North–South long-timers have a similar situation: they are less likely to say they have someone to count on (73%) than the native-born (80%) and are also less likely to say so than if they had stayed in their home country. Long-timers are also less satisfied than the native-born with opportunities to meet people.

Chapter 4
Dimensions of migrant well-being:
Evidence from the Gallup World Poll
156

Figure 33 Social network support and level of interaction with friends and family, among migrants and the native-born, on the four migration pathways, 2009–2011

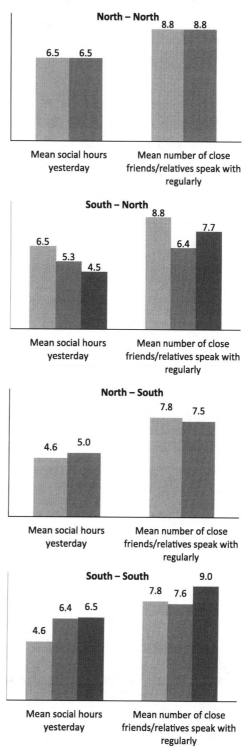

Survey questions put to Gallup poll respondents: Approximately how many hours did you spend socially with friends or family yesterday? About how many close friends or relatives do you speak to at least once every two weeks?

North – North

6.5 6.5 — Mean social hours yesterday
8.8 8.8 — Mean number of close friends/relatives speak with regularly

South – North

6.5 5.3 4.5 — Mean social hours yesterday
8.8 6.4 7.7 — Mean number of close friends/relatives speak with regularly

North – South

4.6 5.0 — Mean social hours yesterday
7.8 7.5 — Mean number of close friends/relatives speak with regularly

South – South

4.6 6.4 6.5 — Mean social hours yesterday
7.8 7.6 9.0 — Mean number of close friends/relatives speak with regularly

Native-born   Long-timers   Newcomers

Source: Gallup World Poll, 2009–2011.
Notes: 1) North–North and North–South newcomers have been excluded due to low sample size.
2) Data have been adjusted by age, sex and education.

 Figure 34   **Opportunities to meet people and the presence of close friends and relatives at home and abroad, among migrants and the native-born, on the four migration pathways, 2009–2011**

Survey questions put to Gallup poll respondents: In the city or area where you live, are you satisfied or dissatisfied with the opportunities to meet people and make friends? If you were in trouble, would you have relatives or friends you can count on to help you whenever you need them, or not? Do you have relatives or friends who are living in another country whom you can count on to help you when you need them, or not?

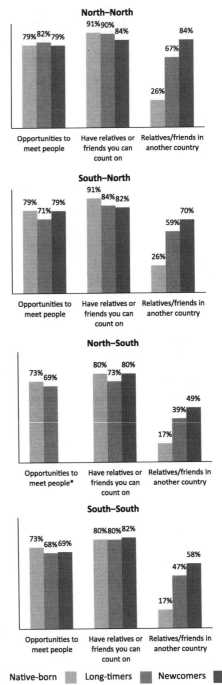

Source: Gallup World Poll, 2009–2011.

Notes: 1) Newcomers have been excluded due to low sample size.
2) Percentages indicate affirmative responses.
3) Data have been adjusted by age, sex and education.

Chapter 4
Dimensions of migrant well-being:
Evidence from the Gallup World Poll 158

Physical well-being

Attempts to assess the state of a country's overall health usually involve the accumulation of health-related statistics, such as life expectancy, infant mortality, and disease infection rates. Additionally, many governments collect health data via surveys of their own residents. Less numerous are survey projects that collect consistent health-related data from respondents across several countries and, in most cases, such multinational efforts focus more on developed countries.

Gallup measures physical well-being worldwide by studying people's perceptions of their own personal health. Gallup also measures people's satisfaction with access to good-quality health care and the likelihood of their having health or medical insurance. People with a high level of physical well-being tend to be more optimistic about their future and about their evaluative well-being.

Key points

- Migrants in the North are as likely as native-born populations to be satisfied with their personal health and the availability of good-quality health care, while migrants in the South rate these aspects lower than do the native-born.

- With the exception of North–North migrants, all other migrants are less likely than the native-born to have health insurance (in addition to statutory insurance).

- Migrants who move from South to North show a gain on all health-related dimensions, compared with matched stayers, while those who move from South to South show a loss.

Satisfaction with personal health

Migrants who have moved to the North report being as satisfied as the native-born in destination countries with the availability of good-quality health care, especially over time. Migrants who have moved to the South are less satisfied than the native-born with their personal health and have more health problems.

In the North, migrants and the native-born share similar perceptions of their health and are similarly satisfied with the availability of good-quality health care in their communities. North–North migrants are as likely as the native-born to have health/medical insurance (in addition to statutory insurance), while those who come from the South are significantly less likely than the native-born to have this insurance. However, over time, health coverage improves (by 35% for newcomers and by 49% for long-timers, compared with 62% for the native-born) (see figure 35).

In the South, migrants are less satisfied than the native-born with their personal health and are more likely to have health problems that keep them from taking part in activities that people their age would normally engage in. While migrants who move from South to North are more likely to get health insurance, with time, no such improvement is evident among migrants who move from South to South.

Are migrants better off, in terms of personal health, than if they had stayed at home?

Comparing long-timers' lives with the hypothetical lives of matched stayers, it appears that all migrants who move to the North experience greater satisfaction with their personal health, the available health care, and the prevalence of insurance. But migrants who move from South to South show a loss on all measured health-related aspects; North–South migrants show a similar pattern, but to a lesser extent (see figure 36).

 Figure 35   Extent of health problems, degree of satisfaction with personal health and available health care, and medical insurance coverage, among migrants and the native-born, on the four migration pathways, 2009–2011

Survey questions put to Gallup poll respondents: Do you have any health problems that prevent you from doing any of the things that people your age normally do? Are you satisfied or dissatisfied with your personal health? In the city or area where you live, are you satisfied or dissatisfied with the availability of quality health care? Do you, personally, have health or medical insurance in addition to statutory health insurance?

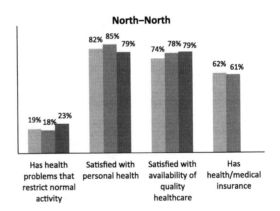

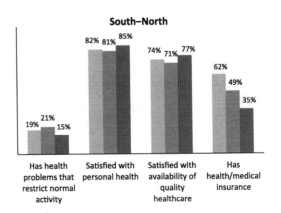

Chapter 4
Dimensions of migrant well-being:
Evidence from the Gallup World Poll   160

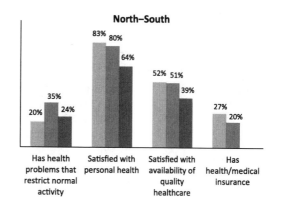

North–South

Has health problems that restrict normal activity: 20%, 35%, 24%

Satisfied with personal health: 83%, 80%, 64%

Satisfied with availability of quality healthcare: 52%, 51%, 39%

Has health/medical insurance: 27%, 20%

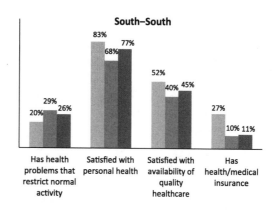

South–South

Has health problems that restrict normal activity: 20%, 29%, 26%

Satisfied with personal health: 83%, 68%, 77%

Satisfied with availability of quality healthcare: 52%, 40%, 45%

Has health/medical insurance: 27%, 10%, 11%

Native-born   Long-timers   Newcomers

Source: Gallup World Poll, 2009–2011.

Notes: 1) Newcomers have been excluded, due to low sample size.

2) Percentages indicate affirmative responses.

3) Data have been adjusted by age, sex and education.

 Figure 36   Extent of health problems, degree of satisfaction with personal health and available health care, and medical insurance coverage, among long-timers and matched stayers, on the four migration pathways, 2009–2011

Survey questions put to Gallup poll respondents: Do you have any health problems that prevent you from doing any of the things that people your age normally do? Are you satisfied or dissatisfied with your personal health? In the city or area where you live, are you satisfied or dissatisfied with the availability of quality health care? Do you, personally, have health or medical insurance in addition to statutory health insurance?

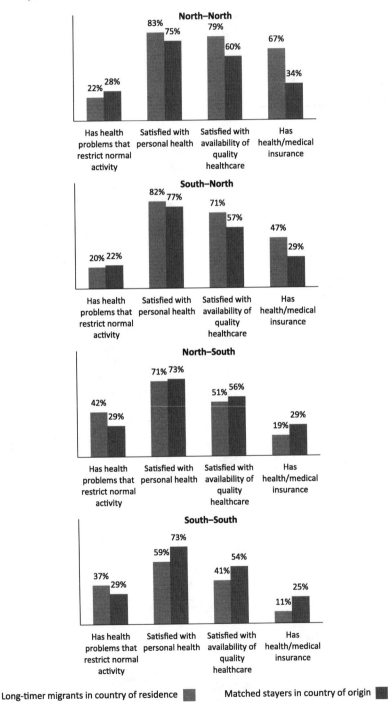

Long-timer migrants in country of residence ▪   Matched stayers in country of origin ▪

Chapter 4
Dimensions of migrant well-being:
Evidence from the Gallup World Poll   162

Source: Gallup World Poll, 2009–2011.
Note: Percentages indicate affirmative responses.

Box 8

Children's well-being

Migrants in the North are more positive about children's opportunities than are the native-born in destination countries, but this is not the case for migrants in the South.

While children's well-being is not one of the five aspects of well-being assessed in the poll, it is quite possible that migrants are thinking of their children's future when responding to questions about their own. Their responses to questions about their own lives are consistent with their responses about children's lives in the destination countries. Gallup finds that, in general, people who live in the North – native-born, newcomers and long-timers – are more optimistic than those in the South about children being treated with respect and having the opportunity to learn and grow.

Migrants living in the North are more positive than the native-born about children's opportunities. However, newcomers are more positive than long-timers, suggesting that migrants' initial optimism diminishes, over time. The patterns are dramatically different in the South: migrants are less optimistic than native-born residents about respect and opportunities for children, and long-timer migrants generally have lower scores than the native-born and the newcomers.

Chapter 4
Dimensions of migrant well-being: 164
Evidence from the Gallup World Poll

 **Figure 37** Perceptions relating to opportunities for children to learn, the treatment of children, and the potential for getting ahead in life by working hard, among migrants and the native-born, on the four migration pathways, 2009–2011

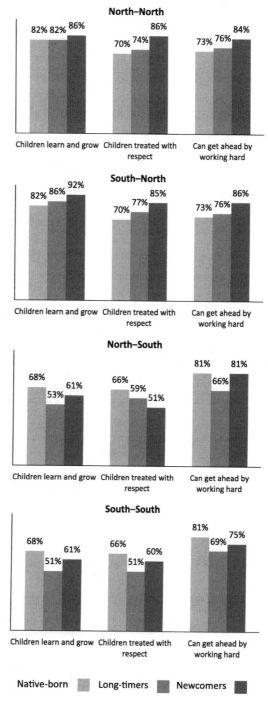

Survey questions put to Gallup poll respondents: Do most children in [country name] have the opportunity to learn and grow every day, or not? Do you believe that children in [country name] are treated with respect and dignity, or not? Can people in this country get ahead by working hard, or not?

Source: Gallup World Poll, 2009–2011.
Notes: 1) Percentages indicate affirmative responses.
2) Data have been adjusted by age, sex and education.

Box 9

Gallup sample

Sample size
This chapter is based on the results from Gallup World Poll surveys in 150 countries and areas in 2009, 2010 and 2011. The typical sample size was 1,000 per country per year. A total of 466,689 adults were included in the analysis, including 441,901 native-born residents and 24,788 first-generation migrants.

Migrant definitions
Each sample was defined by country of birth and duration of stay:

Country of origin questions distinguish migrants from the native-born, and all respondents are asked whether they were born in the country in which they are interviewed. Those born abroad are asked to give their country of birth. Gallup categorizes migrants as "from the North" or "from the South", based on their country of birth and using the World Bank classification.

Duration of stay is determined by asking each respondent identified as a first-generation migrant by the Gallup World Poll to indicate whether he or she moved to the country within the last five years. This way, migrants are divided into two categories: 'newcomers', who moved to their destination country less than five years ago, and 'long-timers', who have been living in their current country for at least five years. These two groups mirror how migrants are commonly classified in census data.

Based on responses to these variables, and using the World Bank classification for North and South, the sample was divided into the following 10 comparison groups:

		MIGRANTS				NATIVE-BORN
		Destination				
		North		South		
		Duration of stay				
		< 5 years	≥ 5 years	< 5 years	≥ 5 years	
Origin	North	North–North Newcomers	North–North Long-timers	North–South Newcomers	North–South Long-timers	North Native-born Residents
	South	South–North Newcomers	South–North Long-timers	South–South Newcomers	South–South Long-timers	South Native-born Residents

Age (in years) was measured as a continuous variable. However, because of extreme values at the higher end of the distribution, age was broken down into several categories.

Sex was measured as male or female, as recorded by the interviewer.

Chapter 4
Dimensions of migrant well-being:
Evidence from the Gallup World Poll 166

<u>Educational achievement</u> was measured on different scales for each country, based on the educational system of the country in question. However, for the global analysis, education was assessed as a three-category variable: primary school or less; some secondary school through three years of tertiary education; and the equivalent of a four-year bachelor's degree or higher education.

 Box 10

Methodology notes

Weighting: Gallup World Poll data are weighted for age, sex and education within a country, to make the country-level data representative of the country's demographic distribution on these variables. Additional weighting is performed so that each country's data are proportional to the total world population.

Migrants and the native-born – controlling for demographics: Well-being measures correlate with demographics (namely, age, sex and education) so multivariate regression techniques were employed to allow for the effects of these demographics and to examine the marginal influence of migrant status on well-being. For continuous dependent variables, a multivariate linear model was employed using SAS's Proc GLM. Age, sex and education were held constant as covariates in a model, and estimated marginal means were obtained to compare the migrant and local groups after controlling for age, sex and education. For categorical dependent variables, multivariate logistic regression was employed with age, sex and education as covariates. All results presented in this report are adjusted for respondents' age, sex and education status.

Migrants and matched stayers – imputation method: The purpose of this analysis was to compare migrants to similar people in the migrants' home country, to extrapolate how the migrants themselves would have fared on the various outcome measures if they had remained in their country of birth. A predicted score was calculated for each migrant that would best represent their response to a question, taking into account their home country and the effect of their age, sex and education in their home country. For each outcome variable:

i) The migrants' own country of birth average score on a given outcome measure was taken as the intercept for that country's migrant's predicted score.

ii) An age, sex and education coefficient was calculated for each country for each variable in order to estimate the effects of demographics on a variable in a country.

iii) The intercept and the age, sex and education coefficient were then combined in a linear equation using the individual migrant's age, sex and education to estimate as closely as possible the migrant's predicted response, given their country of origin, and the effect of age, sex and education on a variable in a country.

This imputation was performed in SPSS using Multiple Imputation Techniques, which maintains the variance of the predicted scores similar to the variance of the actual scores. Once each migrant respondent was assigned an actual and predicted score, paired t-tests were used to determine statistically significant differences in the experiences of migrants in their country of residence, compared to what their experiences would have been like if they had remained in their country of birth.

Sample coverage: Gallup's migrant sample population includes regular and irregular migrants, but does not distinguish further between them or isolate subcategories of migrants, such as victims of trafficking, unaccompanied minors, refugees or stranded migrants. The Gallup sample does not identify return migrants; it excludes migrants who may reside in group situations such as refugee camps; and it excludes non-Arab expatriates in Gulf Cooperation Council countries. Additionally, because Gallup conducts interviews in each country's most common languages, migrants who do not speak the languages used for the surveys in each country may be under-represented.

Aggregation of data collected in different periods: While some core measures were collected every year during this period (2009, 2010, 2011), some were collected only for one or two years. Some data from different years were aggregated to ensure adequate sample size for each subgroup. The analysis of subgroup samples with fewer than 200 respondents are not included in this report.

CONCLUDING REMARKS

Few migration and development studies focus on the movement of people from richer countries in the North to poorer countries in the South, or on the movement of people between countries in the South. Most studies on migration tend to focus on the situation of migrants in the North. Gallup's data provide, for the first time, a global picture of the experience of migrants, shedding light on the often-understudied migrants in the South.

The large sample sizes of migrants afforded by Gallup's World Poll enable researchers to investigate the well-being of migrants – not just in the North or the South, but across all four migration pathways. Thirty-three per cent of migrants included in Gallup's sample have moved from South to South, and 5 per cent moved from North to South; 40 per cent moved from South to North, and 22 per cent moved from North to North.

It is generally assumed that most people move voluntarily in search of a better life. Indeed, a recent report from UNDP concluded that: "the majority of movers end up better off – sometimes much better off – than before they moved [...] and that the gains are greatest for people who move from poor to the wealthiest countries" (UNDP, 2009:29). One study found that: "on average, migrants to OECD countries had a Human Development Index (HDI) score of about 24 per cent higher than that of people who stayed in their respective countries of origin" (UNDP, 2009:67). However, this study did not distinguish between North–North and South–North migration.

Chapter 4
Dimensions of migrant well-being:
Evidence from the Gallup World Poll   168

Findings from the Gallup World Poll are based on how migrants assess their own well-being. The Gallup results illustrate how migrants worldwide face different challenges, each with advantages and disadvantages, depending on the direction of their migration flow. Length of stay in a destination country plays a big role in migrants' well-being. What might be vital to a newcomer who has lived in their destination country for fewer than five years may be less important for a migrant who has lived there longer. Similarly, perceptions about their current situations and future opportunities change according to their duration of stay in the destination country.

The evidence presented in this report suggests that, across many dimensions, migrants report that they experience less well-being than the native-born residents, even though, in some instances, they may be better off than matched stayers in their country of origin. However, the greatest differences are not between migrants and the native-born in the North, but between migrants and native-born residents in the South.

Overall, migrants are less likely than the native-born to be able to meet their basic needs (namely, to buy the food they need and to obtain adequate shelter); they are more likely to be found in lower-income groups; and they are more likely to be underemployed or unemployed. There are exceptions for some of these aspects of well-being. Migrants in the South are less likely than the native-born to feel safe in the area where they live; migrants in the North, on the other hand, feel as safe as the native-born residents. South–South newcomers are the most vulnerable, when it comes to safety: they are least likely to feel safe and most likely to have been mugged or had property stolen. Migrants in the South are less likely than the native-born to be satisfied with their personal health and the availability of good-quality health care, and they are less likely to have health insurance. Migrants in the North are as likely as the native-born to be satisfied with their personal health and with the availability of good-quality health care.

Gallup found that migrants who move from North to North are more likely to experience greater well-being. This is not to say that migrants moving from South to North do not make significant gains in this area but, in many respects, these migrants report that their well-being is poorer than that of the native-born residents or those who have moved from North to North. For instance, after living in their destination country for more than five years, North–North migrants reach the financial level of the native-born; there is less improvement among South–North migrants. Overall, migrants who have moved from North to North are better off financially than migrants who have moved from South to North.

Since there is no universal approach to improving migrants' well-being, there is a need for new approaches to be developed – not only to improve the personal human development of migrants, but also to potentially raise the development level in both their country of destination and their country of origin.

Next steps – the way forward

These poll findings are a sample of what Gallup has learned from national surveys about migrants' well-being. Additional research is needed for a more complete understanding of the potential relationship between migration and development. The well-being outcomes of migration are greatly affected by the conditions under which people move, but it is not known how migrant well-being varies with different conditions in certain countries or regions. Nor has it been possible to explore in detail the effect of migration on the well-being of different migrant categories, such as labour migrants, students, irregular migrants, trafficked persons, return migrants, or migrants stranded due to conflict situation and environmental disasters.

IOM and Gallup will continue to pursue new avenues of migrant-related research. Leveraging its established network of global resources, Gallup can conduct more focused studies with different migrant groups, such as irregular migrants, return migrants, migrant diaspora, and displaced persons. These types of resources, for example, enabled Gallup to conduct its World Poll surveys in camps of people displaced by the devastating earthquake in Haiti. Diasporas, which already have established links to development in both country of destination and country of origin, represent another relevant target group to be mapped and studied. Gallup can find clues to help policymakers maximize the relationship between migration and development on both sides, by further studying migrants' working conditions (such as whether they have safe working environments and are working at or below their desired capacity) and by assessing migrants' levels of civic engagement and community attachment.

Gallup also has the research capabilities in major countries of origin to investigate additional microdata-based policy indicators, such as changes in the physical, financial, career, community and social aspects of well-being in households with migrants who are currently abroad – for example, comparing the situation before and after a migrant has left; how remittances are being spent and whether money earned is actually aiding development; and the skills, knowledge and experiences that returning migrants bring back home).

At the global level, migration has not been fully integrated into the global development framework. When countries are asked to report on the progress they have made towards the achievement of development goals such as the Millennium Development Goals (MDGs), there is little mention of migration. This is partly because international migration data currently tell us very little about the well-being of migrants, and the extent to which human development outcomes for migrants are improving.

There is now a great deal of focus on the post-2015 development/MDG agenda and the future shape of the global development framework. How will the global community measure progress towards development in the future? Will the focus shift from objective indicators, such as poverty, mortality and fertility rates, to the broader concept of well-being?

The Gallup World Poll has the potential to provide the international community with better and timely indicators of migrant well-being. This information could, where country samples are large enough, complement other sources of data on migration and development, such as remittances. In this way, the Gallup World Poll could provide the international community with much better indicators of human development outcomes for migrants in the future.

Chapter 4
Dimensions of migrant well-being:
Evidence from the Gallup World Poll 170

Chapter 5

Conclusions

Frank Laczko and Gervais Appave

In 2013, a second High-level Dialogue (HLD) on International Migration and Development will be held,[51] presenting the international community with a valuable opportunity to focus its attention on how to make migration a positive factor in sustainable development and poverty reduction. The HLD 2013 comes at an important time, as the international community considers moving beyond the Millennium Development Goals, and towards the formulation of a new post-2015 development agenda.

The way the international community thinks about migration and its contribution to development has changed significantly over the last decade or so. At the turn of the century, debates about the linkages between migration and development had already captured the interest of the academic community but policymakers had yet to address the issue. In 1999, for example, in a special issue of the *International Migration* journal, focusing on migration and development, Stephen Castles observed pertinently that:

> Many policymakers still see international migration more as a threat to national security and identity than as an opportunity for cooperation and development. There is no 'international community' with common goals and interests in this area as yet (IOM, 1999:16).

In 2000, the international community agreed on a set of Millennium Development Goals (MDGs), but no thought was given to how migration might contribute to the achievement of the MDGs, nor was migration factored into the MDG monitoring framework. Change was in the making, however. In that same year, IOM published its first *World Migration Report (WMR)*, highlighting the many ways in which migration could have both positive and negative impacts on source and destination countries. It pointed out that, globally, USD 77 billion had been sent back to countries of origin in the form of remittances in 1997 (whereas, in 2012, that figure had risen to an estimated USD 529 billion) (World Bank, 2013). The 2000 *WMR* also cited the example of Lesotho – a country for which remittances represented about 50 per cent of the GDP.

Since then, much progress has been made. In 2006, the United Nations General Assembly convened its first-ever High-level Dialogue on International Migration and Development. This event is now seen as a turning point in the international discourse on international migration – the moment at which the international community acknowledged both that migration was an unavoidable reality and that it could benefit both the countries and the migrants concerned. HLD participants drew attention to the global character of the phenomenon and noted that it was growing in both scope and complexity. They went on to affirm that "international migration could be a positive force for development in both countries of origin and countries of destination, provided that it was supported by the right set of policies".

51 The first High-level Dialogue on International Migration and Development was held in 2006.

One key outcome of the HLD was the establishment of a government-led but broadly inclusive global consultative process – the Global Forum on Migration and Development – that has met annually since 2007. Participants include governments, international organizations, non-governmental organizations, academia and the private sector. As the name implies, the GFMD's main objective is to explore the multiple linkages between migration and development. In keeping with the informal, non-binding character of the process, no attempt is made to achieve consensus on policy approaches, but each conference is an opportunity for participants to improve their understanding of issues, to identify available policy responses and discuss best practices. Despite these advances in dialogue and, to a lesser extent, in cooperation at the global level, migration remains inadequately mainstreamed into development frameworks and broader sectoral policies, both at the national and local levels and in global development agendas. A recent survey conducted in 2011, for example, within the framework of a UNDP/IOM project on mainstreaming migration into national development planning, found that few countries have mainstreamed migration into national development plans or instruments (IOM/UN DESA, "Migration and Human Mobility", May 2012). Furthermore, migration policies do not ensure adequate protection of the human rights of all migrants, and public perceptions of migrants and migration have not kept pace with the reality of human mobility and are often inclined to be negative (see IOM's World *Migration Report 2011*).

The 2013 HLD on International Migration and Development presents the international community with a timely opportunity to reflect on progress since the first HLD and to address these gaps in a spirit of multilateral cooperation. The key features and messages of *WMR 2013* are presented as a contribution to this event. They are grouped below under five key headings.

PLACING MIGRANTS AT THE CENTRE OF THE DEBATE

From time immemorial, human beings have migrated in search of a better life. The factors driving migration are numerous and complex: many migrate in search of greater opportunities – to earn a better living, to live in a more agreeable environment or to join family or friends abroad. Of course, a significant number of migrants do not move of their own free will but are forced to do so – refugees escaping persecution, for instance; people devastated by conflict or natural disaster; or victims of trafficking. But those who choose to migrate are driven, first and foremost, by human aspirations. The most fundamental questions they must ask themselves, therefore, are whether they will be happier if they migrate and whether their life will be better than it is now.

For reasons that are quite understandable, however, much research and a great deal of policy debate focus on migration as a process and on its socioeconomic impacts in aggregate terms. Many reports on migration and development focus on the broad socioeconomic consequences of migratory processes through the study of the impact of, for instance, remittances, migrant knowledge networks, or diaspora resources. From this perspective, the consequences of migration for the lives of individual migrants can easily be overlooked. This *World Migration Report 2013* focuses instead on migrants as *persons* and on how the migration experience has affected their lives in positive or negative ways. The approach is consistent with one of the major recommendations of *WMR 2013* – namely that, instead of being the passive subjects of enquiry, migrants should be given the opportunity to tell their stories. This emphasis on the experiential dimension, as opposed to the usual focus on disembodied socioeconomic dynamics, could open the door to policymaking that is more attuned to human needs.

DEVELOPMENT IS ABOUT HUMAN WELL-BEING

A second distinctive feature of this report is its approach to the assessment of development-related outcomes of migration in the context of human well-being. This approach is consistent with recent new orientations in thinking about development that are not limited to notions such as productivity, wealth or income. In a groundbreaking report, *Mismeasuring our Lives: Why GDP Doesn't Add Up*, Stiglitz, Sen and Fitoussi (2010) point out that, for example, GDP can be an inadequate measure of societal progress, given that a country can simultaneously experience an increase in economic activity *and* a decline in life expectancy. The 1986 Declaration on the Right to Development defines development as a "constant improvement of the well-being of the entire population and of all individuals".[52] Similarly, the United Nations Millennium Declaration focuses on the well-being of the individual as the key purpose of development. More recently, the United Nations argued that the notion of well-being and sustainability should be at the core of the global development framework beyond 2015 (UN DESA, 2012a).

While the research community has shown increasing interest in developing and testing instruments to measure societal progress from the perspective of human well-being, a quick review of this work reveals that few studies have focused on the well-being of migrants. Those that exist have focused on only one dimension – measures of happiness – and in just a handful of developed countries.

The *WMR 2013* draws upon the findings of the Gallup World Poll, using data collected in 2009–2011 from 25,000 first-generation migrants and over 440,000 native-born individuals in over 150 countries, to assess, for the first time, the well-being of migrants worldwide. Most studies on migration tend to focus on the situation of migrants in the North. Gallup's data provide, for the first time, a global insight into the experience of migrants, providing new evidence of the often understudied situations of migrants in the South.

Two characteristics of the idea of 'well-being' used in the Gallup Poll need to be underlined. First, well-being is sometimes confused with notions of happiness, but it is a much broader, multidimensional concept. It includes facets of life or life contexts as diverse as health, income, social relationships, security, work and the environment. Second, well-being is considered to have interconnected objective and subjective aspects. The Gallup World Poll assesses the overall well-being of migrants by asking them questions about objective elements in their lives, such as income, shelter and work, as well as subjective perceptions, feelings and impressions of satisfaction with their lives.

52 www.un.org/documents/ga/res/41/a41r128.htm.

MIGRATION IS NOT JUST A SOUTH–NORTH PHENOMENON

Traditionally, migration reports and policy discussions about the contribution of migration to development focus on movements from low- and middle-income countries to more affluent ones (such as from the Philippines to the United States). The *WMR 2013* takes a more inclusive approach and sets out to explore whether variations in the origin and destination of migrants can produce different outcomes for those concerned. In addition to South–North migration, therefore, the report covers three other patterns of movement: migration from one high-income country to another (such as from the United Kingdom to Canada: North–North); migration from a high-income to a low- or middle-income country (such as from Portugal to Brazil: North–South); and migration from one low- or middle-income country to another (such as from Indonesia to Malaysia: South–South). It argues, on the basis of the research findings, that all four 'migration pathways' have consequences for development that are yet to be fully understood and need to be taken into account.

The figures illustrate why a more inclusive way of looking at migration and development is called for. Only a minority of migrants move from South to North – some 40 per cent, according to Gallup sources. At least one third of migrants move from South to South (although the figure could be higher if more accurate data were available), and just over a fifth of migrants (22%) migrate from North to North. A small but growing percentage of migrants (5%) migrate from North to South. These figures can vary somewhat, depending on which definition of 'North' and 'South' is used.

In this report and, broadly speaking, 'North' refers to high-income countries and 'South' to low- and middle-income countries. Clearly, such broad labels have their limitations, given that North and South encompass a wide range of different migrant situations and categories. It is therefore no surprise that different organizations tend to come up with different clusters, depending on their research interests or operational needs. Nonetheless, the terms 'North' and 'South' are widely understood by decision makers. As such, they help provide an understanding of patterns of movement and, consequently, whether the direction of movement has an influence on the well-being of those who have moved.

MIGRATION IMPROVES HUMAN DEVELOPMENT, BUT MANY MIGRANTS STILL STRUGGLE TO ACHIEVE SATISFACTORY LEVELS OF WELL-BEING

Comparing the well-being of migrants with that of similar people in the country of origin

This report provides a unique picture of the gains and losses associated with migration. Drawing on the findings of the Gallup World Poll, it examines what migrants have gained and lost through migration, comparing the well-being of migrants who have lived in a destination country for at least five years with estimates of what their lives might have been like had they stayed at home. It is important to keep in mind, however, that certain vulnerable groups of migrants, such as victims of trafficking, stranded migrants and undocumented migrants, are not identified in the Gallup World Poll.

The greatest gains are associated with migration to the North – whether North–North migration or South–North. Nearly two thirds (62%) of all migrants surveyed by Gallup reside in the North. Interestingly, however, North–North migrants are much more likely than South–North migrants to report that they are better off than they would have been back home. The reverse might have been expected, given the income disparity between the South and the North.

Migrants in the North generally rate their lives better than do their counterparts in the countries of origin. Long-timer South–North migrants (persons living in a country for five years or more), for example, consider themselves to be better off than they would be back home. By contrast, migrants in the South tend to rate their lives as similar to, or worse than, those of 'matched stayers' in the home country (persons of a similar profile who did not migrate). Consequently, South–South long-timers consider themselves to be worse off than if they stayed in their home country – reporting, for example, difficulties in obtaining adequate housing, with 27 per cent of them having struggled to afford shelter in the previous year, compared to 19 per cent of their counterparts back home. Migrants from the South generally report that they have more difficulty in achieving a satisfactory standard of living and do not appear to be better off than if they had stayed at home.

Explaining such differences is not easy and will require further research, but likely factors are higher housing costs in the destination country, less family support, and the fact that migrants in the South tend to be less skilled than those in the North. Given the higher wages and incomes in the North, it is to be expected that South–North migrants will see a bigger improvement in their economic situation than migrants moving from South to South. However, the Gallup survey results indicate that those moving from South to North also gain across a range of other non-economic dimensions, such as health and personal security. Those who move to the North, for example, are much more likely to say that they feel safe walking alone at night than are matched stayers in their home country. In addition, migrants who move to the North report greater satisfaction with their personal health and access to good-quality health care, whereas South–South migrants report reduced well-being, in terms of their health.

Comparing the well-being of migrants with that of the native-born

Although migration brings gains, many migrants in both the North and the South report lower well-being than the native-born, across a number of different dimensions.

Migrants in the South tend to be the least optimistic about their lives and find it difficult to achieve a satisfactory standard of living. Migrants in the South are less likely than the native-born to report that they are satisfied with their lives. South–South long-timers, for example, are the least likely to say that they are happy and enjoying life, with just over half (53%) indicating that they were happy a lot, the day before the survey. South–South migrants also report that they are less well off, financially, than the native-born.

Migrants in the North also face many challenges, but North–North migrants are much less likely than South–North migrants to be struggling to meet their basic needs. Overall, migrants who have moved from North to North consider themselves to be better off, financially, compared to natives, than do migrants who have moved from South to North. The financial situation of migrants in the North is generally not as good as that of the native-born but it improves with time – with 12 per cent of South–North long-timers, for instance, finding it very difficult to get by on their incomes, compared to only 6 per cent of the native-born.

The poor financial situation of migrants is likely linked to their difficulties in obtaining work or, if employed, obtaining a full-time job. Migrants in the North are more likely to be unemployed or underemployed: 26 per cent are underemployed and 13 per cent are unemployed (compared with 18% and 8%, respectively, of the native-born). In the South, migrants are less likely than the native-born to be part of the official workforce, and just as likely as the native-born to be underemployed or unemployed.

Migrants in the South are less likely than the native-born to feel safe in the area where they live (whereas migrants in the North generally feel as safe as native-born residents). Less than half (44%) of South–South newcomers actually feel safe walking alone at night. In the South, migrants are much more likely to report incidents of theft and assault; for example, South–South newcomers are twice as likely as native-born residents to have been mugged (13% compared to 6%). They are also more likely to have had property stolen (23% compared to 15%). For a minority of migrants in the South, fear and high crime rates form real barriers to their full social and economic participation. However, the situation does seem to improve the longer migrants stay in their new country. One explanation for this could be that new migrants historically tend to initially establish themselves in low-income urban areas that have higher crime rates.

Migrants who have moved to or between countries in the South are less satisfied than the native-born with their personal health and are more likely to have health problems that prevent them from taking part in activities that people their age would normally engage in.

To sum up, migrants moving between two high-income countries – or North to North – report the most satisfactory experiences. These migrants have the most positive outcomes in multiple dimensions of well-being, such as life satisfaction, emotional positivity, financial gain, personal safety, community attachment and health. Those migrating between the North and the South, in either direction, have mixed experiences. Generally, economic factors play a notable role: those migrating from the North to the South enjoy greater economic prowess and the ability to make their money go further in a relatively cheaper environment. But North–South migrants tend to have fewer social contacts and are less likely to have someone they can count on for help. Conversely, those moving from the South to the North suffer from this economic differential, struggling to make the transition, but they are nevertheless better off for having migrated than those who stayed at home.

WAY FORWARD AND POST-2015: DEVELOPING A GLOBAL BAROMETER OF MIGRANT WELL-BEING

The shape of the global development agenda beyond 2015 is unknown, but there is growing debate about whether and how migration should be factored into this agenda. How migration could be integrated into this new framework will depend partly on whether the new agenda continues to focus on poverty eradication in the poorest countries of the world, rather than on a broader vision of inclusive and sustainable development for all countries.

Whatever approach is taken, it is evident that there will be a need for a much stronger evidence base to better reflect the linkages between migration and development. Currently, when countries are asked to report on the progress they have made towards the achievement of development goals such as the MDGs, there is hardly any mention of migration, partly due to a lack of data and relevant indicators.

For a better understanding of the implications of migration for human development in the future, better indicators of migrant well-being and additional research are needed. Existing international migration data currently tell us very little about the well-being of migrants, and whether human development outcomes for migrants are improving or not.

The poll findings presented in the *WMR 2013* are only a sample of the information that can be gathered through a global survey. By adding new questions to the existing survey, or by increasing the sample of migrants in certain countries, much more could be learned about the well-being of migrants worldwide. It would be possible, using the Gallup World Poll, to develop an ongoing 'Global Migration Barometer' survey to regularly monitor changes in the well-being of migrants across the globe.

There is much to learn about how migrant well-being varies under different conditions in particular countries or regions – for example, the effect of migration on the well-being of different migrant categories, such as labour migrants, students, irregular migrants, return migrants, or migrants stranded due to conflict situations or environmental disasters. There is a particular need for more evidence regarding the well-being of migrants in the South and the factors shaping their living conditions. More data on emerging trends, such as North–South migration, are also needed for a better understanding of the implications for development.

 **Migrant Voices**

Migrant returns home to Chad in the aftermath of the Libyan crisis (South–South)

Achta was born in Mossoro, Chad in 1975. At the age of 15, as a single mother facing a critical social and financial situation, Achta decided to move to Libya. In her words: "Like many Chadians at that time, I decided to migrate to Libya to find a job, a better life and earnings to support my family – especially my little girl. I had to leave my father and mother behind in a very desperate situation."

Arriving in Libya, Achta initially had difficulty finding a job: "It takes time to learn Libyan Arabic and to learn the Libyan attitude and way of life," she says. But soon Achta began working as a market trader, selling clothes and other items in Benghazi and other cities in Libya.

For Achta, as for many other Chadian migrants, the idea of returning to Chad did not cross her mind until the Libyan crisis started in February 2011: "We never thought about coming back to Chad, one day, since we were happy in Libya, and we were transferring a good portion of our income to support our families and their communities in our villages in Chad," she explains. Achta was in Benghazi when the crisis began. "We were woken up one morning by a very loud sound in front of our house. All of a sudden, we saw a group of armed men on board several vehicles heading towards our house and trying to set it on fire. They kicked us out of the house. Some of them went beyond that to mistreat us and curse us, telling us to leave their country or they were going to kill us. They claimed that we Chadians were big supporters of Gaddafi and that our community was full of mercenaries sent by the Chadian Government to help Gaddafi."

Together with a large group of Chadian migrants – mainly women and children – Achta headed towards Tripoli along the routes she had travelled as a market trader. However, because of insecurity along the road, the usual day-long journey took a week. "We had very little food and water with us and were very worried about the uncertain future," remembers Achta.

"At this point, the majority of the Chadian migrants in Libya were convinced that the situation was not going to end soon and that we had to return home," she says. Assisted by IOM, the United Nations and humanitarian organizations, Achta arrived safely in Chad, along with thousands of others. She is now trying to start a business but, in the meantime, without a job, it is a struggle to care for her five children.

Achta is one of nearly 800,000 migrants who fled Libya, and one of over 200,000 sub-Saharan Africans who returned to their home countries in response to the unrest that began in Libya in February 2011.

Note: Adapted from a presentation by Achta at the International Dialogue on Migration No. 21 Protecting migrants during times of crisis: Immediate responses and sustainable strategies. 13 and 14 September 2012, Geneva.

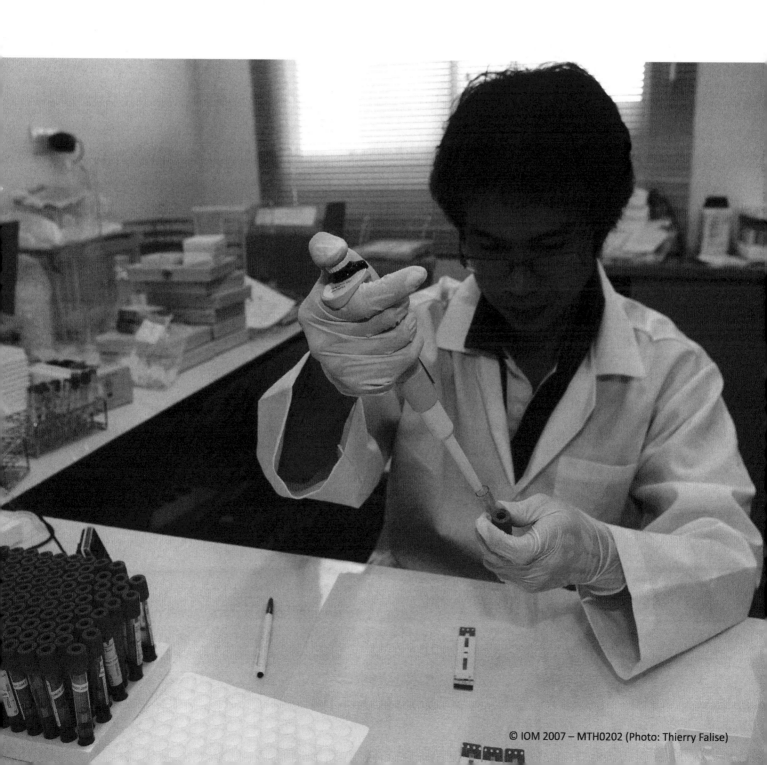

Bibliography

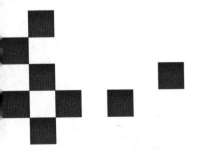

African Development Bank

2012   *African Economic Outlook, Angola 2012*. Available from www.africaneconomicoutlook.org/fileadmin/uploads/aeo/PDF/Angola%20Full%20PDF%20Country%20Note.pdf.

Akay, A. and P. Martinsson

2011   Does relative income matter for the very poor? Evidence from rural Ethiopia. *Economics Letters*, 110(3):213–15.

American Airlines

2012   *American Airlines Applies for Additional Brazil Frequencies*. Available from http://phx.corporate-ir.net/phoenix.zhtml?c=117098&p=irol-newsArticle&ID=1696602&highlight=.

Amit, K.

2010   Determinants of life satisfaction among immigrants from western countries and from the FSU in Israel. *Social Indicators Research*, 96(3):515–34.

Associates for International Research, Inc. (AIRINC)

2011   *2011 Mobility Outlook Questionnaire*. Available from www.air-inc.com.

Aycan, Z. and J.W. Berry

1996   Impact of employment-related experiences on immigrants' psychological well- being and adaptation to Canada. *Canadian Journal of Behavioural Science*, 28(3):240–51.

Ayers, R.L.

1998   *Crime and Violence as Development Issues in Latin America and the Caribbean*. World Bank, Washington, D.C.

Badal, S.

2010   *Entrepreneurship and Job Creation: Leveraging the Relationship*. Gallup Press, Washington, D.C.

Badal, S. and R. Srinivasan

2011   Mentor support key to starting business. *Gallup World*, 11 November 2011. Available from www.gallup.com/poll/150974/Mentor-Support-Key-Starting-Business.aspx.

Bakewell, O.

2009   *South–South Migration and Human Development: Reflections on African Experiences*. Human Development Research Paper 2009/07, UNDP, New York. Available from http://hdr.undp.org/en/reports/global/hdr2009/papers/HDRP_2009_07.pdf.

Balkır, C. and B. Kırkulak

2009   Turkey, the new destination for international retirement migration. In: *Migration and Mobility in Europe Trends, Patterns and Control* (H. Fassmann et al., eds). Edward Elgar Publishing: Cheltenham, UK and Northampton, USA.

Ball, R. and K. Chernova

2008   Absolute income, relative income, and happiness. Social Indicators Research, 88(3):497–529.

Bartram, D.

2010   International migration, open borders debates, and happiness. *International Studies Review*, 12(3):339–61.

2011   Economic migration and happiness: comparing immigrants' and natives' happiness gains from income. *Social Indicators Research*, 103(1):57–76.

2012a   Happiness and 'Economic Migration': A comparison of Eastern European Migrants and Stayers. *Social Science Research Network* (SSRN) E-library. Available from http://ssrn.com/abstract=2225679.

2012b   Migration, return, and happiness in Romania. *European Societies* (forthcoming).

Bechetti, L. et al.

2008   Relational goods, sociability, and happiness. *Kyklos*, 61(3):343–363.

Bergheim, S.

2006   Measures of Wellbeing: There is more to it than GDP. *Deutsche Bank Research – Global Growth Centres*. Available from www.dbresearch.com/PROD/DBR_INTERNET_EN-PROD/PROD0000000000202587.PDF.

Bernstein, N. and E. Dwoskin

2007   Brazilians giving up their American dream. *New York Times*, 4 December 2012. Available from www.nytimes.com/2007/12/04/nyregion/04brazilians.html?pagewanted=all&_r=0.

Berry, J.W.

1997   Immigration, acculturation, and adaptation. *Applied Psychology*, 46(1):5–34.

Blanchflower, D.G. and A.J. Oswald

2004   Well-being over time in Britain and the USA. *Journal of Public Economics*, 88(7–8):1359–86.

2005   Happiness and the human development index: the paradox of Australia. *Australian Economic Review*, 38(3):307–18.

Boarini, R. et al.

2006   *Alternative Measures of Well-Being. OECD Social, Employment and Migration Working Papers*, 33. Organisation for Economic Co-operation and Development (OECD), Paris.

2012   *What Makes for a Better Life? The Determinants of Subjective Well-being in OECD Countries – Evidence from the Gallup World Poll*. OECD Statistics Working Papers, 2012/03. OECD Publishing, Paris.

Boehm, J.K. and S. Lyubomirsky

2008   Does happiness promote career success? *Journal of Career Assessment*, 16(1):101–16.

Borraz, F. et al.

2007   And what about the family back home? International migration and happiness. Paper presented to Public Policy Development Office Conference, Bangkok.

Boyce, C.J. et al.

2010   Money and happiness: rank of income, not income, affects life satisfaction. *Psychological Science*, 21(4):471–75.

BP

2010   *BP in Angola Sustainability Report 2010*. BP, London.

Brazier, M. (ed.)

2012   *Global Mobility Survey Report 2012: Exploring the Changing Nature of International Mobility*. Commissioned by the Santa Fe Group and undertaken by Circle Research, London.

Brülde, B.

2010   Happiness, morality, and politics. *Journal of Happiness Studies*, 11(5):567–83.

Bureau of Immigration (Philippines)

2011a *Foreign Tourists Opting to Stay Longer in PHL – BI*, 23 August 2011. Bureau of Immigration, the Philippines, Manila. Available from http://immigration.gov.ph/index.php?option=com_content&task=view&id=1080&Itemid=78.

2011b *Koreans topped the list of foreign students in RP*. 18 March 2011. Bureau of Immigration, the Philippines, Manila. Available from http://immigration.gov.ph/index.php?option=com_content&task=view&id=692&Itemid=78.

2012 *61,000 foreign students studying in RP*. 9 February 2012. Bureau of Immigration, the Philippines, Manila. Available from http://immigration.gov.ph/index.php?option=com_content&task=view&id=1420&Itemid=78.

Cai, R., N. Esipova and M. Oppenheimer

2012 The effects of subjective well-being on international migration intention. Working paper. Unpublished.

Cardenas, M. et al.

2009 Migration and life satisfaction: evidence from Latin America. *Journal of Business Strategies*, 26(1):9–26.

Carens, J.H.

1992 Migration and morality: a liberal egalitarian perspective. In: *Free Movement: Ethical Issues in the Transnational Migration of People and of Money* (B. Barry and R.E. Goodin, eds). Harvester Wheatsheaf, London, pp. 25–47.

Cassarino, J. (ed.)

2008 *Return Migrants to the Maghreb Countries: Reintegration and Development Challenges*. European University Institute, Florence. Available from http://cadmus.eui.eu/bitstream/handle/1814/9050/MIREM%20_General_Report_2008.pdf?sequence=1.

Clark, A.E. and A.J. Oswald

1994 Unhappiness and unemployment. *The Economic Journal*, 104(424):648–59.

Clark, A.E. et al.

2008 Relative income, happiness and utility: an explanation for the Easterlin paradox and other puzzles. *Journal of Economic Literature*, 46(1):95–144.

Clifton, J. and J. Marlar

2011 *Good Jobs: The New Global Standard*. Gallup, Inc., Washington, D.C.

CNN Money

2011   American workers seek jobs in Asia. *CNN Money*, 17 May 2011. Available from http://money.cnn.com/video/news/2011/05/17/n_americans_jobs_asia.cnnmoney/.

Conceição, P. and R. Bandura

2008   *Measuring Subjective Wellbeing: A Summary Review of the Literature.* United Nations Development Programme (UNDP) Development Studies Research Papers. UNDP, New York.

Córdova, R.

2012   *Rutas y dinámicas migratorias entre los países de América Latina y el Caribe (ALC), y entre ALC y la Unión Europea [Migration routes and dynamics between the countries of Latin America and the Caribbean (LAC), and between LAC and the European Union].* International Organization for Migration (IOM), Geneva.

Correa, M. C.

2011   *Hooked on Korea: Understanding Korean Pop Culture in the Philippines.* Ateneo de Manila University.

2012   When Philippine TV got ROK-ed. *ASEAN-Korea Centre blog*, 2 April 2012. Available from http://blog.aseankorea.org/archives/11030.

Cox, R. and T. Sinclair

1996   *Approaches to World Order.* Cambridge University Press.

Csikszentmihalyi, M.

1997   *Finding Flow: The Psychology of Everyday Life.* Basic Books, New York.

Cullen, L. T.

2007   The New Expatriates. *TIME Magazine – Business*, 24 September 2007. Available from www.time.com/time/magazine/article/0,9171,1670516,00.html.

Deaton, A.

2008   Income, health, and well-being around the world: evidence from the Gallup World Poll. *Journal of Economic Perspectives* 22(2):53–72;

Deaton, A., J. Fortson and R. Tortora

2010   *International Differences in Wellbeing.* Oxford University Press, Oxford/New York.

Department of Tourism – Philippines

n.d.   Visitor statistics: arrivals by country of residence. Available from www.visitmyphilippines.com/index.php?title=VisitorStatistics&func=all&pid=39&tbl=1.

De Prycker, V.

2010   Happiness on the political agenda? Pros and cons. *Journal of Happiness Studies*, 11(5):585–603.

Diener, E. et al.

1985   The satisfaction with life scale. *Journal of Personality Assessment*, 49(1):71.

1999   Subjective well-being: three decades of progress. *Psychological Bulletin*, 125(2):276-303.

2009a   *Well-Being for Public Policy*. Oxford University Press, Oxford.

2009b   A primer for reporter and newcomers. Available from http://internal. psychology.illinois.edu/~ediener/faq.html#SWB.

Dixon, D. et al.

2006   *America's Emigrants: US Retirement Migration to Mexico and Panama*. Migration Policy Institute (MPI), Washington, DC. Available from www.migrationinformation.org/feature/display.cfm?ID=416.

Dolan, P. et al.

2008   Do we really know what makes us happy? A review of the economic literature on the factors associated with subjective well-being. *Journal of Economic Psychology*, 29(1):94–122.

2011   *Measuring Subjective Well-being for Public Policy*. Office for National Statistics, London.

Dreby, J.

2010   *Divided By Borders: Mexican Migrants and their Children*. University of California Press, Berkeley.

Dumont, J-C. et al.

2010   *International Migrants in Developed, Merging and Developing Countries: an Extended Profile*. OECD Social Employment and Migration Working Papers, No.114. Organisation for Economic Co-operation and Development (OECD), Paris. www.oecd.org/migration/internationalmigrationpoliciesanddata/46535333.pdf.

Duncan, G.

2010   Should happiness-maximization be the goal of government? *Journal of Happiness Studies*, 11(2):163–78.

Easterlin, R.A.

1974   Does economic growth improve the human lot? In: *Nations and Households in Economic Growth: Essays in Honor of Moses Abramowitz* (P.A. David and M.W. Reder, eds). Academic Press, New York, pp. 89–125.

1995   Will raising the incomes of all increase the happiness of all? *Journal of Economic Behavior and Organization*, 27:35–47.

2001   Income and Happiness: Towards a Unified Theory. *The Economic Journal*, 111(473):465–84.

2003   Explaining happiness. *Proceedings of the National Academy of Sciences*, 100(19):11176–83.

Easterlin, R.A. et al.

2010   The happiness-income paradox revisited. *Proceedings of the National Academy of Sciences*, 107(52):22463–68.

Eichhorn, J.

2011   Happiness for believers? Contextualizing the effects of religiosity on life-satisfaction. *European Sociological Review*.

Ellerman, D.

2005   Labour migration: a development path or low-level trap? *Development in Practice*, Vol. 15, 5 (2005):617–630.

Embassy of the Republic of Korea

2012   *Korea Bulletin*, January 2012. Available from http://embassy_philippines.mofat.go.kr/english/as/embassy_philippines/mission/notice/index.jsp.

Emigration Observatory (*Observatório da Emigração*)

n.d.   Países de destino da emigração portuguesa: Angola [Destination countries for Portuguese migrants: Angola]. Available from www.observatorioemigracao.secomunidades.pt/np4/home.html (accessed in March 2013).

Entorf, H. and H. Spengler

2000   *Criminality, social cohesion, and economic performance. Wuerzburg Economic Papers*, No. 00–22.

Esipova, N. et al.

2011   The European migrant experience. Paper presented at the OECD Working Party on Migration. 9–10 June 2011. Available from www.gallup.com/strategicconsulting/158144/european-migrant-experience-gallup-working-paper-presented-oecd.aspx.

Eurostat

2010   *Demography Report 2010: Older, more numerous and diverse Europeans*. Available from http://epp.eurostat.ec.europa.eu/cache/ITY_OFFPUB/KE-ET-10-001/EN/KE-ET-10-001-EN.PDF.

Firebaugh, G. and M.B. Schroeder

2009   Does your neighbor's income affect your happiness? *American Journal of Sociology*, 115(3):805–31.

Fix, M. et al.

2009   *Migration and the Global Recession: A Report Commissioned by the BBC World Service*. Migration Policy Institute, Washington, D.C.

Frank, R.H.

1999   *Luxury Fever: Money and Happiness in an Era of Excess*. Princeton University Press, Princeton.

Frey, B. and A. Stutzer

2002   *Happiness and Economics: How the Economy and Institutions Affect Human Well-being*. Princeton University Press, Princeton.

Gagnon, J. and D. Khoudour-Castéras (eds)

2011   Immigrant integration in the South. In: *Tackling the Policy Challenges of Migration Regulation, Integration, Development*. OECD Publishing, Paris.

Gallup

2012   *Worldwide Research Methodology and Codebook 2012*. Gallup, Washington, D.C.

Gartaula, H. et al.

2012   Socio-cultural dispositions and wellbeing of the women left behind: a case of migrant households in Nepal. *Social Indicators Research*, forthcoming.

Garutti, C. et al.

2009   *Brazil and China: Immigration and Visas*. EMDOC, São Paulo, Brazil.

Gilbert, D.

2006   *Stumbling on Happiness*. HarperCollins, New York.

Global Forum for Migration and Development (GFMD)

2012   *Addressing South–South Migration and Development Policies*. Background paper prepared by the International Organization for Migration (IOM) and the ACP Observatory for the GFMD Roundtable 2.2. Available from www.gfmd.org/documents/mauritius/gfmd12_mauritius12_rt_2-2-background_paper_en.pdf.

Global Migration Group (GMG)

2010 *Mainstreaming Migration into Development Planning: A Handbook for Policy-makers and Practitioners*. International Organization for Migration (IOM), Geneva.

Goodin, R.E.

1998 Permissible paternalism: in defense of the nanny state. In: *The Essential Communitarian Reader* (A. Etzioni, ed.). Rowman & Littlefield, Lanham, pp. 115–23.

Gough, I. and J. A. McGregor (eds)

2007 *Wellbeing in Developing Countries: From Theory to Research*. Cambridge University Press, Cambridge.

Graham, C.

2005 Insights on development from the economics of happiness. *The World Bank Research Observer*, 20(2):201–31.

2008 Happiness and health: lessons – and questions – for public policy. *Health Affairs*, 27(1):72–87.

2009 *Happiness Around the World: The Paradox of Happy Peasants and Miserable Millionaires*. Oxford University Press, Oxford.

2011 *The Pursuit of Happiness: Toward an Economy of Well-Being*. Brookings Institution Press, Washington, D.C.

Graham, C. and J. Markowitz

2011 Aspirations and happiness of potential Latin American immigrants. *Journal of Social Research and Policy*, 2(2):9–25.

Gravelle, T. et al.

2010 *What makes 700 million adults want to migrate*. Gallup, Washington, D.C.

Haller, M. and M. Hadler

2004 Happiness as an Expression of Freedom and Self-determination. In: *Challenges for Quality of Life in the Contemporary World* (W. Glatzer, S. Von Below and M. Stoffregen (eds), Kluwer, London, pp. 207–232.

Handlin, O.

1973 *The Uprooted*. Little Brown & Company, New York.

Haybron, D.M.

2008 *The Pursuit of Unhappiness: The Elusive Psychology of Well-Being*. Oxford University Press, Oxford.

Helliwell, J. et al. (eds)

2012 *World Happiness Report*. The Earth Institute, Columbia University.

Horst, C., J. Carling and R. Ezzati

2010   *Immigration to Norway from Bangladesh, Brazil, Egypt, India, Morocco and Ukraine.* Peace Research Institute Oslo (PRIO). Available from http://file.prio.no/Publication_files/Prio/Immigration%20 to%20Norway,%20PRIO%20Policy%20Brief%202010.pdf.

Hugo, G.

2005   *Migration in the Asia-Pacific Region.* A paper prepared for the Policy Analysis and Research Programme of the Global Commission on International Migration. Available from www.iom.int/jahia/webdav/ site/myjahiasite/shared/shared/mainsite/policy_and_research/ gcim/rs/RS2.pdf.

Huff-Hannon, J.

2009   Hard days for a buff and shine man, *New York Times*, 6 February 2009. Available from www.nytimes.com/2009/02/08/nyregion/ thecity/08braz.html.

Huppert, F.A., N. Baylis and B. Keverne (eds)

2006   *The Science of Well-being.* Oxford University Press, Oxford, pp. 285– 304.

Inglehart, R.

1997   *Modernization and Postmodernization. Cultural, Political and Economic Change in 43 Societies.* Princeton University Press, Princeton.

Instituto Brasileiro de Geografia e Estatística (IBGE)

2012a   Migracão [Migration]. In: *Censo Demográfico 2010: Resultados gerais da amostra* [*Demographic Census 2010: Overall Results of the Sample*]. IBGE [Brazilian Institute of Geography and Statistics], Rio de Janeiro. Available from ftp://ftp.ibge.gov.br/Censos/Censo_ Demografico_2010/Resultados_Gerais_da_Amostra/resultados_ gerais_amostra.pdf.

2012b   2010 Census: Schooling and income increase and infant mortality falls. Available from http://censo2010.ibge.gov.br/en/noticias-censo ?view=noticia&id=1&idnoticia=2125.

2012c   *Main Highlights in the evolution of the Labour Market 2003–2011* [*Principais destaques da evolução do mercado de trabalho 2003– 2011*]. IBGE, Rio de Janeiro. Available from www.ibge.gov.br/ english/estatistica/indicadores/trabalhoerendimento/pme_nova/ defaultestudos.shtm.

Instituto Nacional de Estadística (INE) (Portugal)

2012   Data taken from the database of Instituto Nacional de Estadística (INE) [Statistics Portugal]. Available from www.ine.pt/xportal/xmain?xlang=pt&xpgid=ine_main&xpid=INE (data extracted in October 2012).

Instituto Nacional de Estadística (INE) (Spain)

2012   Data taken from the database of the Instituto Nacional de Estadística (INE) [National Statistics Institute], Spain. Available from www.ine.es/ (data extracted in November 2012).

Ip, M.

2012   Here, there, and back again: A New Zealand case study of Chinese circulatory transmigration. *Migration Information Source*, Migration Policy Institute, Washington, D.C. Available from www.migrationinformation.org/Feature/display.cfm?id=878.

International Monetary Fund (IMF)

2012   *World Economic Outlook*. Available from www.imf.org/external/pubs/ft/weo/faq.htm#q4b.

International Organization for Migration (IOM)

1999   Migration and Development. *International Migration*, Quarterly review, Vol. 37 No. 1, Special Issue. Blackwell Publishing Ltd, Oxford/Malden, MA.

2010a   *Migration, Employment and Labour Market Integration Policies in the European Union – Part 1: Migration and the Labour Markets in the European Union (2000–2009)*. IOM, Brussels.

2010b   *Migration profile of Brazil 2009*. IOM, Geneva.

2012   *Crushed Hopes: Underemployment and deskilling among skilled migrant women*. IOM, Geneva. Available from http://publications.iom.int/bookstore/index.php?main_page=product_info&cPath=41_7&products_id=892.

International Organization for Migration (IOM) and Migration Policy Institute (MPI)

2009   Perfil Migratório do Brasil [Migration Profile of Brazil]. IOM, Geneva. http://publications.iom.int/bookstore/index.php?main_page=product_info&cPath=41_42&products_id=632.

2012   *Developing a Road Map for Engaging Diasporas in Development: A Handbook for Policymakers and Practitioners in Home and Host Countries*. IOM, Geneva/MPI, Washington, DC. Available from http://publications.iom.int/bookstore/index.php?main_page=product_info&products_id=787.

International Organization for Migration (IOM) and United Nations Department for Economic and Social Affairs (UN DESA)

2012   *Migration and Human Mobility: Thematic Think Piece*. United Nations System Task Team on the Post-2015 UN Development Agenda. Available from www.un.org/en/development/desa/policy/untaskteam_undf/them_tp.shtml.

Jasinskaja-Lahti, I. et al.

2006   Perceived discrimination, social support networks, and psychological well-being among three immigrant groups. *Journal of Cross-Cultural Psychology*, 37(3):293–311.

Kahneman, D. and J. Riis

2005   Living, and thinking about it: two perspectives on life. In: *The science of well-being*. (F.A. Huppert, N. Baylis and B. Keverne (eds). Oxford University Press, Oxford, pp. 285–304.

Kahneman, D. et al.

2004   A survey method for characterizing daily life experience: the day reconstruction method. *Science*, 306(5702):1776–80.

Kenny, C.

2005   Does development make you happy? Subjective wellbeing and economic growth in developing countries. *Social Indicators Research*, 73(2):199–219.

2011   *Getting Better: Why Global Development Is Succeeding, and How We Can Improve the World Even More*. Basic Books, New York.

Knight, J. and R. Gunatilaka

2010   Great expectations? The subjective well-being of rural-urban migrants in China. *World Development*, 38(1):113–24.

Lee, H.

2012   From the Ambassador's desk. *Korea Bulletin*, April 2012, No. 46. Available from http://embassy_philippines.mofat.go.kr/english/as/embassy_philippines/mission/notice/index.jsp.

Legarda, L.

2011   Speech of Senator Loren Legarda. Second Philippines–Korea Partnership Forum, Intercontinental Hotel, Makati City, 5 December 2011. Available from www.lorenlegarda.com.ph/speeches_065_2nd_philippines_korea_partnership_forum.php.

Lemaitre, G.

2005 The Comparability of International Migration Statistics: Problems and Prospects," *Statistics Brief*, July 2005, No. 9. OECD, Paris. Available from www.oecd.org/migration/internationalmigrationpoliciesanddata/36064929.pdf.

Lora, E. and J.C. Chaparro

2009 The Foreign National in Brazil: Legislation and Comments. Fourth Edition. EMDOC, São Paulo. Available from www.brasilglobalnet.gov.br/ARQUIVOS/Publicacoes/Manuais/PUBEstrangeiroNoBrasil.pdf.

Lima, D. et al.

2009 The conflictive relationship between satisfaction and income. In: *Paradox and Perception: Measuring Quality of Life in Latin America* (C. Graham and E. Lora, eds). Brookings Institution Press, Washington, D.C. pp. 57–95.

Lucas, R.E. et al.

2003 Reexamining adaptation and the set point model of happiness: reactions to changes in marital status. *Journal of Personality and Social Psychology*, 84(3):527–39.

2004 Unemployment alters the set point for life satisfaction. *Psychological Science*, 15(1):8–13.

Lykken, D. and A. Tellegen

1996 Happiness is a stochastic phenomenon. *Psychological Science*, 7(3):186–89.

Malheiros, J.

2010 Portugal 2010: o regresso do país de emigração? Notas e reflexões [Portugal 2010: returning to a country of emigration? Reflections and notes]. *JANUS.NET e-journal of International Relations*, Vol. 2, No, 1, spring 2011. Available from http://observare.ual.pt/janus.net/images/stories/PDF/vol2_n1/pt/pt_vol2_n1_not3.pdf.

Martiz, J.

2012 Talent grab: How top companies are managing Africa's skills shortage. *How We Made it in Africa*. 5 March 2012. Available from www.howwemadeitinafrica.com/talent-grab-how-top-companies-are-managing-africas-skills-shortage/15372/.

McGillivray, M.

2007   Human well-being: issues, concepts and measures. In: *Well-being –* *Concept and Measurement* (M. McGillivray, ed.). Palgrave Macmillan, New York. Available from www.palgrave.com/pdfs/0230004989.pdf.

Meinardus, R.

2005   The 'Korean Wave' in the Philippines. *The Korea Times*, 15 December 2005. Available from www.fnf.org.ph/liberalopinion/korean-wave-in-the-philippines.htm.

Melzer, S.M.

2011   Does migration make you happy? The influence of migration on subjective well-being. *Journal of Social Research and Policy*, 2(2):73–92.

Ministry of Labour and Employment (MTE)

2012   *Base Estatística Geral – Detalhamento das autorizações concedidas* *em 2012* [General Statistics Database – breakdown of work permits issued in 2012]. Available from http://portal.mte.gov.br/geral/estatisticas.htm (accessed in March 2013).

Miralao, V.

2007   Understanding the Korean diaspora in the Philippines. In: *Exploring* *Transnational Communities in the Philippines* (V. Miralao and L. Makil, eds). Philippine Migration Research Network and Philippine Social Science Council, Quezon City. Available from http://unesdoc.unesco.org/images/0015/001530/153053e.pdf.

Miralao, V. and L. Makil (eds),

2007   *Exploring Transnational Communities in the Philippines.* Philippine Migration Research Network and Philippine Social Science Council, Quezon City. Available from http://unesdoc.unesco.org/images/0015/001530/153053e.pdf.

Moreira, H.

2006   Portuguese emigration (Retrospective statistics and thematic reflections). Instituto Nacional de Estadística (INE), p. 47. Available from www.ine.pt/xportal/xmain?xpid=INE&xpgid=ine_estudos&ESTUDOSest_boui=56468797&ESTUDOSmodo=2.

Murray, K., G. Davidson and R. Schweitzer

2008   *Psychological Wellbeing of Refugees Resettling in Australia: A* *Literature Review Prepared for The Australian Psychological Society.* Available from www.psychology.org.au/assets/files/refugee-lit-review.pdf.

National Bureau of Statistics of China

2001   *Communiqué on Major Figures of the 2000 Population Census (No. 1)*. 28 March 2001. Available from www.stats.gov.cn/was40/ gjtjj_en_detail.jsp?searchword=population+census&channelid=9528 &record=20.

2011   *Communiqué of the National Bureau of Statistics of People's Republic of China on Major Figures of the 2010 Population Census (No. 1)*. 28 April 2011. Available from www.stats.gov.cn/english/ newsandcomingevents/t20110428_402722244.htm.

Neto, F.

1995   Predictors of satisfaction with life among second generation migrants. *Social Indicators Research*, 35(1):93–116.

Oishi, S.

2010   Culture and well-being: conceptual and methodological issues. In: *International Differences in Well-Being* (E. Diener et al., eds). Oxford University Press, Oxford, pp. 34–69.

Organisation for Economic Co-operation and Development (OECD)

2007   *Jobs for Immigrants (Vol. 1): Labour Market Integration in Australia, Denmark, Germany and Sweden*. OECD Publications, Paris. Available from www.oecd.org/els/mig/ jobsforimmigrantsvol1labourmarketintegrationinaustraliadenmark germanyandsweden.htm.

2010a *Perspectives on Global Development 2010: Shifting Wealth*. OECD Development Centre, Paris.

2010b Education at a Glance 2010: OECD Indicators. Available from http:// browse.oecdbookshop.org/oecd/pdfs/free/9610071e.pdf.

2010c *Entrepreneurship and Migrants*, Report by the OECD Working Party on SMEs and entrepreneurship. OECD Publications, Paris.

2011   *How's Life?: Measuring Well-being*. OECD Publications, Paris.

2012a *International Migration Outlook 2012*. OECD Publications, Paris. Available from http://dx.doi.org/10.1787/migr_outlook-2012-en.

2012b Fourth World Forum on Statistics, Knowledge and Policy: Measuring Well-Being for Development and Policy Making, 16–19 October 2012. New Delhi, India.

Ono, M.
2008   Long-stay tourism and international retirement migration: Japanese retirees in Malaysia. *Transnational Migration in East Asia: Senri Ethnological Reports*, 77:151–162.

O'Reilly, K. and M. Benson (eds)
2009   Lifestyle migration: Escaping to the good life? In: *Lifestyle migration: Expectations, Aspirations and Experiences*. Farnham, Ashgate, Chapter 1.

Papadopoulos, G.
2012   The relationship between immigration status and victimization: evidence from the British Crime Survey. Presented at the European Economic Association & Econometric Society 2012 Parallel Meetings, 27 August 2012.

Park, A. et al.
2010   Shock and recovery in China's labour market: Flexibility in the face of a global financial crisis. CEA Conference on Global Economic Recovery: the Role of China and Other Emerging Economies, University of Oxford, 12–13 July 2010.

Passel, J., D. Cohn and A. Gonzalez-Barrera.
2012   *Net Migration from Mexico Falls to Zero – and Perhaps Less*. Pew Research Hispanic Center, Washington, D.C.

Pew Research Center
2007   Global Opinion Trends 2002–2007. The Pew Global Attitudes Project. Available from www.pewglobal.org/2007/07/24/chapter-1-global-publics-view-their-lives-2/.

Pieke, F.
2012   Immigrant China. *Modern China*, 38(1):40–77.

Pinto de Oliveira, L.A. and A. T. Ribeiro de Oliveira
2011   *Estudos e análises: Informação demográfica e socioeconômica, numero 1 - Reflexões sobre os deslocamentos populacionais no Brasil [Studies and Analyses: Demographic and Socioeconomic Information, No. 1 – Reflections on displaced populations in Brazil]*. Ministry of Planning, Budget and Management, Instituto Brasileiro de Geografia e Estatística [Brazilian Institute of Geography and Statistics] (IBGE), Rio de Janeiro.

Porter, M. and N. Haslam

2005   Predisplacement and postdisplacement factors associated with mental health of refugees and internally displaced persons: a meta-analysis. *Journal of the American Medical Association*, 294(5):602–612. Available from http://jama.jamanetwork.com/article. aspx?articleid=201335#REF-JRV50016-4.

Prilleltenskzy, I.

2008   Migrant well-being is a multilevel, dynamic, value dependent phenomenon. *American Journal of Community Psychology*, 42(3-4):359-364. Available from www.springerlink.com/content/v611611865362x3l/.

Pugliese, A. and J. Ray

2011   Three Percent Worldwide Get International Remittances. *Gallup World*, 6 May 2011. Washington DC. Available from www.gallup.com/poll/147446/Three-Percent-Worldwide-International-Remittances. aspx.

Ratha, D. and W. Shaw.

2007   *South–South Migration and Remittances*. World Bank Working Paper, No. 102. World Bank, Washington, DC. Available from http://siteresources. worldbank.org/INTPROSPECTS/Resources/334934-1110315015165/ SouthSouthMigrationandRemittances.pdf.

Rath, T. and Harter, J.

2010   *Wellbeing: The Five Essential Elements*. Gallup Press, New York, NY.

Reuveny, R. and W. Thompson

2007   The North–South divide and international studies: A symposium. *International Studies Review*, 9 (2007):556–564.

Rios-Neto, E.

2005   *Managing Migration: The Brazilian Case*. Discussion Paper No. 249. Available from www.cedeplar.ufmg.br/pesquisas/td/TD%20249.pdf.

Royal Government of Bhutan

2012   *The Report of the High-Level Meeting on Wellbeing and Happiness: Defining a New Economic Paradigm*. Thimphu: Office of the Prime Minister, The Permanent Mission of the Kingdom of Bhutan to the United Nations, New York.

Rumbaut, R.G.

1997   Assimilation and its discontents: between rhetoric and reality. *International Migration Review*, 31(4):923–60.

Safi, M.

    2010   Immigrants' life satisfaction in Europe: between assimilation and discrimination. *European Sociological Review*, 26(2):159–71.

Santos, R. and M. Tomeldan

    2006   Case-based study of three tourism-dependent islands in the Philippines: The cases of Boracay Island, Aklan; Puerto Galera, Oriental Mindoro; & Coron, Palawan in the Philippines. *MUHON: A Journal of Architecture, Landscape Architecture and the Designed Environment*, No. 3. Available from http://journals.upd.edu.ph/index.php/muhon/article/viewFile/1319/1288.

Schimmel, J.

    2009   Development as happiness: the subjective perception of happiness and UNDP's analysis of poverty, wealth and development. *Journal of Happiness Studies*, 10(1):93–111.

Schnittker, J.

    2008   Happiness and success: genes, families, and the psychological effects of socioeconomic position and social support. *American Journal of Sociology*, 114:S233–S59.

Scitovksy, T.

    1992   *The Joyless Economy: The Psychology of Human Satisfaction*. Oxford University Press, Oxford.

Self, A., J. Thomas and C. Randall

    2012   *Measuring National Well-being: Life in the UK, 2012*. Office for National Statistics. Available from www.ons.gov.uk/ons/dcp171766_287415.pdf.

Seligson, H.

    2009   American graduates finding jobs in China. *New York Times*, 10 August 2009. Available from www.nytimes.com/2009/08/11/business/economy/11expats.html?pagewanted=all.

Sen, A.

    1992   *Inequality Reexamined*. Oxford University Press, Oxford.

    1999   *Development as Freedom*. Knopf, New York.

Sheldon, K.M. and S. Lyubomirsky

    2006   Achieving sustainable gains in happiness: change your actions, not your circumstances. *Journal of Happiness Studies*, 7(1):55–86.

Simons, A. et al.

1987   *Psychology: The Search for Understanding*. West Publishing Company, New York.

Skeldon, R.

2011   China: an emerging destination for economic migration. *Migration Information Source*, Migration Policy Institute. Available from: www.migrationinformation.org/Profiles/display.cfm?ID=838.

Stark, O.

1991   *The Migration of Labor*. Basil Blackwell, Oxford.

Stevenson, B. and J. Wolfers

2008   *Economic Growth and Subjective Well-being: Reassessing the Easterlin Paradox*. IZA Discussion Paper 3654. Institute for the Study of Labor (IZA), Bonn.

Stiglitz, J., A. Sen and J-P Fitoussi

2009   *Report by the Commission on the Measurement of Economic Performance and Social Progress*. Available from www.stiglitz-sen-fitoussi.fr.

2010   *Mismeasuring our Lives: Why GDP Doesn't Add Up*. New Press, New York/London.

Stutzer, A.

2003   The role of income aspirations in individual happiness. *Journal of Economic Behavior & Organization*, 54(1):89–109.

Sullivan, B.

2011   Move to China for a job? Unemployed cope by leaving US. *The Red Tape Chronicles on NBCNEWS.com*. 11 October 2011. Available from http://redtape.msnbc.msn.com/_news/2011/10/10/8257389-move-to-china-for-a-job-unemployed-cope-by-leaving-us.

Sullivan, O.

1996   The enjoyment of activities: do couples affect each others' well-being? *Social Indicators Research*, 38(1):81–102.

Sussman, N.

2010   *Return Migration and Identity: A Global Phenomenon, a Hong Kong Case*. Hong Kong University Press, Hong Kong. Available http://books.google.ch/books?hl=en&lr=&id=mvcWnjYiq_YC&oi=fnd&pg=PR5&dq=return+migration+of+brazilians&ots=8ALPq-1dKB&sig=Jl4ghqyrwUFTQafC6oJe5miN8Mw&redir_esc=y#v=onepage&q=return%20migration%20of%20brazilians&f=false.

Thérien, J-P

1999   Beyond the North–South divide: the two tales of world poverty. *Third Word Quarterly*, Vol. 20, No. 4 (1999):723–742.

Thompson, S. et al.

2007   *The European (Un)Happy Planet Index: An Index of Carbon Efficiency and Well-being in the EU*. New Economics Foundation, London.

Toyota, M.

2007   Migration of the elderly: emerging patterns in Asia. Presented on 1 October 2007 at the Migration and Development Series Seminar on Migration and Social Security in Ageing World, United Nations Institute for Training and Research, United Nations, New York.

United Nations

2012   *Realizing the Future We Want for All. Report to the Secretary-General*. UN System Task Team on the Post-2015 UN Development Agenda. United Nations, New York. Available from www.un.org/millenniumgoals/pdf/Post_2015_UNTTreport.pdf.

United Nations Conference on Trade and Development (UNCTAD)

2012   *The Least Developed Countries Report 2012: Harnessing Remittances and Diaspora Knowledge to Build Productive Capacities*. UNCTAD, Geneva.

United Nations Department of Economic and Social Affairs (UN DESA), Population Division

2009   *Trends in International Migrant Stock: The 2008 Revision – Philippines Country Profile 1990–2010*. UN DESA, New York. Available from http://esa.un.org/migration/.

2011a   *Trends in international Migration stock: Migrants by Age and Sex, 2011*. UN DESA, New York.

2011b   *World Population Prospects, the 2010 Revision*. File 19: Net number of migrants (both sexes combined) by major area, region and country, 1950–2100. Available from http://esa.un.org/unpd/wpp/Excel-Data/migration.htm; http://esa.un.org/unpd/wpp/index.htm; http://unstats.un.org/unsd/methods/m49/m49.htm; http://unstats.un.org/unsd/methods/m49/m49regin.htm#ftnc (accessed in March 2013).

2012a   *The United Nations Development Strategy Beyond 2015*. Policy Note. Committee for Development Policy, UN DESA, New York.

2012b   *Trends in International Migrant Stock: Migrants by Destination and Origin*. United Nations database, POP/DB/MIG/Stock/Rev.2012.

2012c   Population Facts No. 2012/3, June 2012. Available from www.un.org/esa/population/publications/popfacts/popfacts_2012-3_South-South_migration.pdf.

United Nations Educational, Scientific and Cultural Organization (UNESCO)

n.d.   Data taken from the UNESCO Institute of Statistics (UIS) Data Centre. Available from http://stats.uis.unesco.org/unesco/TableViewer/ document.aspx?ReportId=136&IF_Language=eng&BR_Topic=0 (accessed in March 2013).

2009   *Global Education Digest (GED) 2009: Comparing Education Statistics Across the World.* UNESCO Institute for Statistics (UIS), Montreal.

2011   *Global Education Digest (GED) 2011. Comparing Education Statistics Across the World.* UNESCO Institute for Statistics (UIS), Montreal. Available from www.uis.unesco.org/library/pages/default. aspx?docID=530.

2012   *New Patterns in Student Mobility in the Southern Africa Development Community.* UNESCO Institute for Statistics (UIS) Information Bulletin No. 7, February 2012. Available from www.uis.unesco.org/ FactSheets/Documents/ib7-student-mobility-2012-en.pdf.

United Nations Develoment Programme (UNDP)

n.d.   Human Development Index (HDI). Available from http://hdr.undp. org/en/statistics/hdi/.

2009   *Overcoming Barriers: Human Mobility and Development (Human Development Report 2009).* UNDP/Palgrave, New York.

United Nations General Assembly (UNGA)

2012   *International migration and development, Report of the Secretary-General,* Sixty-seventh session, 31 July 2012, A/67/XXXX, United Nations General Assembly, New York.

United Nations High Commissioner for Refugees (UNHCR)

n.d   UNHCR Statistical Online Population Database. Available from www. unhcr.org/statistics/populationdatabase (data extracted in January 2013).

2013   *Global Trends 2013.* UNHCR, Geneva.

United Nations Statistics Division

2008   *World Population Prospects: The 2008 Revision.* United Nations Statistics Division, UN DESA, New York.

2011   *World Statistics Pocketbook.* Data available online at: http://data. un.org/CountryProfile.aspx?crName=BRAZIL (accessed in March 2013).

United Nations Volunteers

2011   *State of the World's Volunteerism Report 2011: Universal Values for Well-being.* United Nations Volunteers (UNV), Bonn. Available from www.unv.org/fileadmin/docdb/pdf/2011/SWVR/English/ SWVR2011_full.pdf.

US Department of State

2012   *Global Trafficking in Persons Report*. US Department of State, Washington, D.C. Available from www.state.gov/j/tip/rls/tiprpt/2012/.

United States Diplomatic Mission to Brazil

2012   Embassy and Consulates announce February 2012 consular statistics. *United States Diplomatic Mission to Brazil*, 9 March 2012. Available from http://brazil.usembassy.gov/visas/whats-new/embassy-and-consulates-announce-february-2012-consular-statistics.html.

Veenhoven, R.

1984   *Conditions of Happiness*. D. Reidel Publishing Company, Dordrecht.

1991   Is happiness relative? *Social Indicators Research*, 24(1):1–34. 1993 *Happiness in Nations: Subjective Appreciation of Life in 56 Nations, 1946–1992*. Erasmus University, Rotterdam.

Veenhoven, R. and J. Ehrhardt

1995   The cross-national pattern of happiness: test of predictions implied in three theories of happiness. *Social Indicators Research*, 34(1):33–68.

Veronese, G. et al.

2012   My happiness is the refugee camp, my future Palestine: optimism, life satisfaction and perceived happiness in a group of Palestinian children. *Scandinavian Journal of Caring Sciences* (forthcoming).

Wadhwa, V. et al.

2009   *America's Loss Is the World's Gain: America's New Immigrant Entrepreneurs, Part IV*. Kauffman Foundation of Entrepreneurship, Kansas City. Available from http://papers.ssrn.com/sol3/papers.cfm?abstract_id=1348616.

2011   *The Grass Is Indeed Greener in India and China for Returnee Entrepreneurs: America's New Immigrant Entrepreneurs, Part VI*. Kauffman Foundation of Entrepreneurship, Kansas City. Available from www.kauffman.org/uploadedfiles/grass-is-greener-for-returnee-entrepreneurs.pdf.

Wang, N. et al.

2012   Can well-being be measured using Facebook status updates? Validation of Facebook's Gross National Happiness Index. *Social Indicators Research* (forthcoming).

Wright, K.

2011   Constructing Migrant Wellbeing: An Exploration of Life Satisfaction Amongst Peruvian Migrants in London. *Journal of Ethnic and Migration Studies* 37(9):1459–1475. Available from www.tandfonline.com/doi/pdf/10.1080/1369183X.2011.623621.

World Bank (WB)

n.d.   How we classify countries. The World Bank (online data). Available from http://data.worldbank.org/about/country-classifications.

2010   Bilateral Remittance Estimates. World Bank (online data and research). http://econ.worldbank.org/WBSITE/EXTERNAL/EXTDEC/EXTDECPR OSPECTS/0,,contentMDK:22803131~pagePK:64165401~piPK:6416 5026~theSitePK:476883,00.html (World Bank remittance data are estimated using assumptions and arguments as explained in Ratha and Shaw, 2007, *South–South Migration and Remittances*. Available from www.worldbank.org/prospects/migrationandremittances.

2013   *Migration and Development Brief 20*. Migration and Remittances Unit, Development Prospects Group, 19 April.

Yap, D.J.

2011   Filipinos attracted to Korean culture, K-pop, Koreanovelas. *Philippine Daily Inquirer*, 12 December 2011. Available from http://newsinfo. inquirer.net/109439/filipinos-attracted-to-korean-culture-k-pop-koreanovelas.

Glossary of key terms[55]

55 Please see IOM's *International Migration Law No. 25 – Glossary on International Migration: Second Edition* (2011) for a comprehensive list of migration-related terminology.

Brain drain
Emigration of trained and talented persons from the country of origin to another country, resulting in a depletion of skills in the former.

Brain gain
Immigration of trained and talented persons to a destination country. Also called 'reverse brain drain'.

Career well-being
One of Gallup's six dimensions of well-being. Career well-being refers to well-being in the context of career and employment. To assess levels of career well-being, Gallup examines, inter alia, individuals' employment status, their views about their own job situation, and their perceptions of entrepreneurship, including the potential obstacles to setting up a business.

Community well-being
One of Gallup's six dimensions of well-being. Community well-being refers to the quality of one's relationship with the community in which one lives. Gallup gauges community well-being by measuring, inter alia, people's perceptions of their personal safety, their confidence in national institutions, their views on the prevalence of corruption in business and government, and their degree of community attachment.

Country of destination
The country that is a destination for migrants (regular or irregular). See also *host country* and *receiving country*.

Country of origin
Generally speaking, the country of origin refers to the country that was the point of departure for the individual's migratory journey. In chapter 4, however, for purely methodological reasons, this term is used to refer to a migrant's country of birth.

Development
The United Nations Development Programme (UNDP) defines development as the process of "creating an environment in which people can develop their full potential and lead productive, creative lives in accordance with their needs and interests... expanding the choices people have to lead lives that they value". This definition marks a shift away from the strict emphasis on economic development measured by growth or income indicators and encompasses the human dimension of the process.

Diasporas

There is no single accepted definition of the term *diaspora*. Diasporas are broadly defined as individuals and members of networks, associations and communities who have left their country of origin, but maintain links with their homelands. This concept covers more settled expatriate communities, migrant workers temporarily based abroad, expatriates with the citizenship of the host country, dual citizens, and second-/third-generation migrants.

Economic migrant

A person leaving his/her habitual place of residence to settle outside of his/her country of origin in order to improve his/her quality of life. This term is often loosely used to distinguish migrants from refugees fleeing persecution and is also similarly used to refer to persons attempting to enter a country without legal permission and/or by using asylum procedures without bona fide cause. It may equally be applied to persons leaving their country of origin for the purpose of employment.

Evaluative well-being

One of two aspects of subjective well-being, which is part of Gallup's six dimensions of well-being. Evaluative well-being concerns the way individuals remember and assess their past experiences. Gallup assesses evaluative well-being by asking respondents to rate their actual life, overall, and to estimate what their life might be like in five years.

Experiential well-being

One of two aspects of subjective well-being, which is part of Gallup's six dimensions of well-being. Experiential well-being is concerned with momentary affective states and the way people feel about experiences in real time. Gallup assesses experiential well-being by asking respondents about a set of positive and negative feelings that they may experience during the day.

Financial well-being

One of Gallup's six dimensions of well-being. Financial well-being refers to well-being in the context of personal finances and satisfaction with living standards. Gallup assesses individuals' personal economic situations and the situations of the communities in which they live by asking a serious of questions relating to income and the ability to live on that income.

Forced migration

A migratory movement in which there is an element of coercion, including threats to life and livelihood, whether arising from natural or human-made causes (for example, movements of refugees and internally displaced persons, as well as people displaced by natural/environmental disasters, chemical/nuclear disasters, famine or development projects).

High-income countries

In accordance with World Bank country classifications, high-income countries are identified on the basis of gross national income (GNI) per capita. In this report, high-income countries refer to all economies that had a GNI per capita of USD 12,276 or more in 2010. High-income countries have the highest GNIs per capita of any World Bank income group, the others being (in descending order) upper-middle-income, lower-middle-income, and low-income countries. For the purposes of the current report, high-income countries are referred to as 'the North'.

Host country

The country in which a migrant is living. See also *country of destination and receiving country*.

Internal migration

A movement of people from one area of a country to another for the purpose or with the effect of establishing a new residence. This migration may be temporary or permanent. Internal migrants move but remain within their country of origin (as in the case of rural to urban migration). See also *internally displaced persons*.

Internally displaced persons (IDPs)

Persons or groups of persons who have been forced or obliged to flee or to leave their homes or places of habitual residence, particularly as a result, or in order to avoid the effects, of armed conflict, situations of generalized violence, violations of human rights, or natural/human-made disasters, and who have not crossed an internationally recognized State border (para. 2, *Guiding Principles on Internal Displacement*, UN Doc. E/CN.4/1998/53/Add.2).

Irregular migrant

A person who, owing to unauthorized entry, breach of a condition of entry, or the expiry of his or her visa, lacks legal status in a transit or host country. The definition covers, inter alia, those persons who have entered a transit or host country lawfully but have stayed for a longer period than authorized or subsequently taken up unauthorized employment.

Irregular migration

Movement that takes place outside the regulatory norms of the origin, transit and destination countries.

Long-timer (migrant)

As used by the Gallup World Poll, long-timers are migrants who have lived in their destination country for five years or more.

Low- and middle-income countries

In accordance with World Bank country classifications, low- and middle-income countries are identified on the basis of gross national income (GNI) per capita. In this report, low- and middle-income countries refer to all economies that had a GNI per capita of USD 12,275 or less in 2010. Low- and middle-income countries refer to all economies that are not in the high-income group. For the purposes of the current report, low- and middle-income countries are referred to as 'the South'.

Migration corridor

Generally viewed as the migratory pathway between two different countries, whereby individuals born in, or holding the nationality of, a certain country move to another country.

Native-born

An individual who was born in the country in which he or she currently lives.

Newcomer (migrant)

As used by the Gallup World Poll, newcomers are migrants who have lived in their destination countries for fewer than five years.

North

High-income countries, as classified by the World Bank. See *high-income countries*.

Pathways of migration

Specific migratory routes identified with a view to examining global migration patterns – involving, in the case of this report, four migration scenarios: from North to South; from South to North; from South to South; and from North to North. This categorization allows for a more comprehensive analysis of global migration, moving away from the more traditional focus on South–North movements and, to some extent, South–South. See also *North, South, high-income countries, and low- and middle-income countries*.

Physical well-being

One of Gallup's six dimensions of well-being. Physical well-being refers to well-being in the context of physical and mental health. Physical well-being is also seen to be affected by individuals' access to good-quality health care and the likelihood of their having health or medical insurance.

Receiving country

Country of destination (host country). In the case of return or repatriation, it is also the country of origin.

Refugee

A person who, "owing to a well-founded fear of persecution for reasons of race, religion, nationality, membership of a particular social group or political opinions, is outside the country of his nationality and is unable or, owing to such fear, is unwilling to avail himself of the protection of that country" (*Art. 1(A) (2), Convention relating to the Status of Refugees, 80 International Migration Law Art. 1A(2), 1951, as modified by the 1967 Protocol*). In addition to the refugee definition in the *1951 Refugee Convention, Art. 1(2), 1969*, the Organization of African Unity (OAU) Convention defines a refugee as any person compelled to leave his or her country "owing to external aggression, occupation, foreign domination or events seriously disturbing public order in either part or the whole of his country or origin or nationality". Similarly, the 1984 Cartagena Declaration states that refugees also include persons who flee their country "because their lives, security or freedom have been threatened by generalized violence, foreign aggression, internal conflicts, massive violations of human rights or other circumstances [that] have seriously disturbed public order".

Regional Consultative Processes (RCPs)

Non-binding consultative forums, bringing representatives of States and international organizations together at the regional level to discuss migration issues in a cooperative manner. RCPs also allow for the participation of other stakeholders, such as non-governmental organizations or other civil society representatives.

Regular migration

Migration that occurs through recognized, authorized channels. See also *irregular migration*.

Remittances

Monies earned or acquired by non-nationals that are transferred back to their country of origin. More specifically, the International Monetary Fund defines remittances as the sum of compensations of employees and personal transfers from border, seasonal and other short-term workers who are employed in an economy where they are not resident and of residents employed by non-resident entities.

Return migration

The movement of a person returning to his/her country of origin or habitual residence, usually after at least one year in another country. The return may or may not be voluntary.

Retirement migration

Migration of retirees. Some definitions classify retirement migrants based on their age, others on the basis of migrants' participation in the labour force and receipt of retirement income.

Reverse brain drain
See *brain gain*.

Sending country
A country from which a number of residents depart to settle abroad, permanently or temporarily.

Social well-being
One of Gallup's six dimensions of well-being. Social well-being refers to well-being in the context of personal relationships and social networks. Gallup assesses social well-being by asking about migrants' social support structures and opportunities to make friends in the city or area where they live.

Source country
See *sending country*.

South
Refers to upper-middle-income, lower-middle-income and low-income countries, as classified by the World Bank. See *low- and middle-income countries*.

Student migration
There are various definitions of an international student. The UNESCO Institute for Statistics (UIS) defines internationally mobile students as those who study in a foreign country of which they are not a permanent resident – namely, students who have crossed a national or territorial border for the purpose of education and are now enrolled in studies outside their country of origin.

Subjective well-being
One of Gallup's six dimensions of well-being. Subjective well-being encompasses two aspects of well-being: experiential (relating to individuals' momentary affective states) and evaluative (relating to individuals' memories/assessments of feelings/thoughts about their past and future lives). See *evaluative well-being* and *experiential well-being*.

Trafficking in persons
The recruitment, transportation, transfer, harbouring or receipt of persons, by means of the threat or use of force or other forms of coercion, of abduction, of fraud, of deception, of the abuse of power or of a position of vulnerability or of the giving or receiving of payments or benefits to achieve the consent of a person having control over another person, for the purpose of exploitation (Art. 3(a), Protocol to Prevent, Suppress and Punish Trafficking in Persons, Especially Women and Children, supplementing the United Nations Convention against Transnational Organized Crime, 2000).

Unaccompanied minors

Persons under the age of majority who are not accompanied by a parent, guardian or other adult who, by law or custom, is responsible for them.

Victim of human trafficking

A person who is a victim of the crime of trafficking in persons. See also *trafficking in persons*.

Well-being

While there is no single universally recognized conceptualization of well-being, in a broad sense, well-being refers to the quality of an individual's life situation. This report uses the definition developed by Gallup, whose data inform the original research findings on which the report is based. Gallup identifies career satisfaction, quality of social connections, personal economic situation, health and community as the main contributing factors in a person's overall subjective well-being.